Using Interactive Whiteboards in the Classroom

BLUE RIVER ELEMENTARY
LIBRARY MEDIA CENTER

Author
Kathleen Kopp, M.A.

Foreword
Eric LeMoine, M.Ed.

Consultant

James D. Anderson, M.S.Ed.

Contributing Author

Eric LeMoine, M.Ed.

Publishing Credits

Dona Herweck Rice, *Editor-in-Chief*
Robin Erickson, *Production Director*
Lee Aucoin, *Creative Director*
Timothy J. Bradley, *Illustration Manager*
Sara Johnson, M.S.Ed., *Senior Editor*
Aubrie Nielsen, M.S.Ed., *Associate Education Editor*
Grace Alba, *Designer*
Stephanie McGinley, *Photo Editor*
Corinne Burton, M.A.Ed., *Publisher*

Shell Education
5301 Oceanus Drive
Huntington Beach, CA 92649-1030
http://www.shelleducation.com

ISBN 978-1-4258-0779-5

© 2013 Shell Educational Publishing, Inc.

The classroom teacher may reproduce copies of materials in this book for classroom use only. The reproduction of any part for an entire school or school system is strictly prohibited. No part of this publication may be transmitted, stored, or recorded in any form without written permission from the publisher.

Table of Contents

Foreword 5
Chapter 1: The Research Behind the Technology 7
Chapter 2: The Basics of Interactive Whiteboards 25
Chapter 3: Interactive Whiteboards
in the Classroom 39
Chapter 4: Designing Effective Lessons with
Interactive-Whiteboard Technology 59
Chapter 5: Getting Started with the
Interactive Whiteboard 91
Chapter 6: Exploring Advanced Features of the
Interactive Whiteboard 127
Chapter 7: Differentiating Instruction with
Interactive Whiteboards 155
Afterword 179
Appendix A: SMART Notebook™ How-to Guide 181
Appendix B: ActivInspire™ How-to Guide 191
Appendix C: Internet Resources 200
References Cited 208

Foreword

IWB Tips *from an expert*

Instructional Technology Coach and Trainer Eric LeMoine offers tips for implementing interactive whiteboards throughout this book.

Although I embraced many technologies as a classroom teacher in Beaverton, Oregon, my introduction to the world of the interactive whiteboard (IWB) came after I transitioned to a district-level position as a Teacher on Special Assignment in instructional technology. One of my responsibilities in that role was to pilot the introduction of IWBs in elementary, middle, and high schools throughout the district. The purpose of the pilot was twofold: to determine whether one IWB platform might work better for our classrooms than another, and to see for ourselves whether IWB technology brought any benefits to instruction. I took a rather atypical route to build my knowledge of the new technology—I purchased an interactive whiteboard and projector for my home, and then (much to my wife's dismay) mounted it in our family room! This allowed me ample time to learn the technology and experiment with bringing curriculum to the IWB. I quickly realized that the IWB was a fun and engaging tool for both my children and their friends. But I also learned that the real challenge as a teacher was to bring meaningful and authentic *student-centered* experiences to the technology. It was all too easy to use the IWB as a glorified projection surface with the teacher operating the board most of the time. The difficult task is to build lessons and activities that foster student interaction with the board.

Some of the best arguments against the placement of interactive whiteboards into classrooms center around two facts: that many IWBs sit idly in classrooms without much, if any, use; and that IWBs become a teacher-centered tool with students mostly watching from their seats. However, in my current role as an instructional technology coach I have not only learned that professional development and ongoing modeling and support can ensure that IWBs are in constant use, but that the transition from a teacher-centered to a student-centered classroom is advanced by the use of IWB technology.

In this book, Kathleen Kopp provides many ideas to bring the student to the IWB. She also provides many simple yet powerful ways for the teacher to bring authentic, engaging tasks to the IWB that integrate classroom curricula. There are ideas for both the novice and more experienced IWB user. The topic of effective IWB lesson design is addressed with concrete, usable suggestions across the content areas. An entire chapter is dedicated to using the interactive whiteboard to differentiate instruction. Regardless of whether you are a classroom teacher, an on-site instructional technology coach, or a district-level administrator, there are useful ideas for you in this book.

Throughout the book, you will find *IWB Tips from an Expert*. These suggestions and tips come from my experiences as a technology coach in classrooms and from my opportunities as an international trainer and consultant in instructional technology. As I continue to consult as an IWB specialist, I realize that the true experts are the teachers and students whom I have had the privilege of working with at schools across the United States and around the world. They have taught me so much about how interactive whiteboards can motivate, engage, and bring real-world learning experiences to the classroom. Kathleen Kopp has done the same thing for you throughout this book. Whether you are beginning or continuing your IWB journey, I am confident that your practice will be positively influenced by this book.

Happy Reading!

—Eric LeMoine, M.Ed.
Instructional Technology Coach
International Educational Trainer/Consultant

Chapter 1

The Research Behind the Technology

Interactive whiteboards have been welcome additions to classrooms since 1991. This chapter explores the changing role of technology in our students' education, how interactive whiteboards contribute to a "sustainable classroom," and how initial research supports their use in highly effective classrooms.

> **Did You Know?**
>
> By 2009, nearly three million interactive whiteboards had been installed worldwide.

The Future Is Now

Today's classrooms do not look like those of just ten years ago. As advances in technology become more sophisticated and more readily accessible, students benefit from their use in everyday core subjects such as reading, language arts, mathematics, science, and social studies, and in elective courses, such as band, industrial arts, and visual art. States, school districts, and schools are in the midst of the digital age and are continuing to move forward. The Florida legislature passed a law in 2011 requiring school districts to use fifty percent of instructional materials dollars "for the purchase of electronic or digital materials on the state-adopted list by the 2015–16 school year" (Florida Department of Education, 2011). Schools are supplying students with electronic tablets for everyday use. Students at Clearwater High School in Florida had their textbooks replaced with eBook readers at the start of the 2010–2011 school year in an attempt to "integrate more technology with classroom instruction" (Catalanello 2010, 10th paragraph). Cushing Academy, a Boarding School in Ashburnham, Massachusetts, renovated its library in 2009. Included in the renovations, aside from the usual floors and furniture, was a complete replacement of its 20,000 or so text-based resources. Instead, students can access millions of digital books. This complete technological overhaul included flat-panel televisions in the media center, and e-readers and laptops for every student.

Indeed, the digital age is having a profound effect on of our schools. While some schools embrace new technology and pave the way as models for other schools to follow, other schools use what electronic support they can from limited resources. Included in this technology wave is the use of the interactive whiteboard (IWB). Whether students each have a personal tablet or computer or the teacher is the only person in the classroom to have ready access to the digital world, an IWB is a viable instructional tool that teachers can use as part of an effective, technology-rich environment.

The use of interactive whiteboards has grown tremendously over the past several years. According to Corcoran (2009), the sales of SMART™ wall screens increased from 170,000 units in 2004 to 700,000 worldwide in 2009. Most of these sales were to schools. With an increase of sales equal to about 400 percent over the past five years, it is clear that interactive-whiteboard technology is becoming a valuable asset to teachers and students. According to Futuresource Consulting, an independent global research company that has tracked IWB sales for over nine years, twenty percent of classrooms worldwide will have an interactive whiteboard by 2013 (CCP Interactive Blog 2011).

IWBs are part of a "sustainable classroom." According to Educational Service District 112, a sustainable classroom is a "classroom technology integration model that utilizes a broad number of highly visual, interactive technologies with a single computer in order to support the nine instructional strategies that are identified in Marzano's book, *Classroom Instruction that Works* [Marzano, Pickering, and Pollock 2001]" (2011, 2nd paragraph). Interactive whiteboards allow teachers to use technology as a natural part of instruction focused on highly effective instructional strategies. Since only one computer is needed to project software and programs onto the whiteboard, the financial burden of replacing technology is reduced. In addition, once a teacher is trained in the effective use of an interactive whiteboard (which includes ensuring that the IWB is not a teacher-centered tool), the teacher need only hone his or her skills or incorporate software updates as they become available. This reduces the need for specialized training in more advanced technologies. Finally, technical support needs are reduced to only those which support the technology already in the classroom. Since the interactive whiteboard is the mainstay of the instructional practice, technical support need address only the computer, projector, whiteboard, and software updates that are necessary for all the technology to work cohesively and fluidly.

Did You Know?

In 2009, almost one-third of K–12 classes in the United States and three-fourths of the schools in the United Kingdom had an interactive whiteboard.

What the Research Tells Us

Interactive-whiteboard technology has been around less than twenty years. Consequently, the research related to the use of interactive whiteboards is in its infancy when compared to other research on best practices in reading and mathematics instruction. A few researchers have published findings related to the use of IWBs in the classroom, but much of what is available for review is not yet found in peer-reviewed periodicals. All the same, when synthesized collectively, one underlying theme runs true: interactive whiteboards are an effective instructional tool capable of increasing student achievement, especially when integrated with pedagogically sound teaching strategies. In other words, a teacher cannot simply hook up an interactive whiteboard, use it sparingly or for only one function, and expect his or her students' test scores to improve. As with any instructional tool, it is only as effective as the person using it. Therefore, research in this area includes qualifiable data related to instructional best practices, with the interactive whiteboard used effectively to enhance what has been established as sound instruction.

A review of the available research offers information related to several areas of improved classroom performance: student achievement, instructional practices, and student behavior. Two benefits of IWB use are directly related to student outcomes. The third is related to improved instructional practice on the part of the teacher. Regardless of a teacher's motivation for using interactive whiteboards in the classroom setting, when used correctly and effectively, the students will benefit and the teacher will improve his or her own professional practices as well.

Improved Student Achievement

Classroom procedures, instructional materials, and supplemental resources may change at any time of year in today's classrooms. No matter what we bring in or throw out, the overall goal in education never changes: teachers want their students to be successful with the content. They want students to be confident learners and demonstrate their mastery of skills and understanding of concepts in some meaningful way. They want their students to be thoughtful, well-informed, and prepared individuals who are ready to tackle challenges, solve problems, learn from mistakes, and celebrate successes as they come. The effective use of interactive whiteboards can help students reach and exceed their educational objectives.

Recent studies regarding the use of interactive whiteboards in classrooms share similar results; overall, there is little statistically significant difference in achievement in English between students whose teachers use IWBs as part of their daily routine and those whose teachers do not use this technology to support instruction in this subject area. However, studies do suggest that the use of interactive whiteboards in mathematics does lead to statistically significant achievement gains (BECTA 2003; SMART 2006). This does not mean that interactive whiteboard use is ineffective in reading and language arts instruction. IWBs contribute to significant gains in achievement among students in fourth and fifth grades in both reading and mathematics, according to pre- and post-assessment of the Ohio Achievement Test (Swan, Schenker, and Kratcoski 2006). Additionally, the study discovered a link among third- through eighth-grade teachers between the frequency and complexity of a teacher's use of an interactive whiteboard and those who used it sparingly and for limited purposes. Teachers who used their IWB every day (or nearly every day) and for advanced interactive functions had students who scored above the mean on standardized assessments. Advanced functions included visualization of concepts and processes; problem solving; manipulation of figures, charts, and graphs; and the use of published and student-generated interactive math games.

IWB Tips from an expert

Student interaction with IWBs does not always have to be on an advanced level. Second-grade teachers have their students utilize the IWB as an independent station on a daily basis during Daily Five Word Work (Boushey and Moser 2006). One of the students' favorite activities during this time is a relatively simple one: Students are given a list of vocabulary words and are asked to re-create the words by dragging existing letters from a letter bank. After forming each word, students write the word on the IWB with the pen. Although an IWB is not necessary for this type of activity, students are often more engaged when forming their words on the IWB as compared to the same activity without an IWB. They will usually complete more words when using the IWB and more consistently use these words in their subsequent writing activities.

These findings are supported by Somekh et al. in their *Report to the Department for Children, Schools, and Families*: "There is a consistent finding across all data that the length of time pupils have been taught with an interactive whiteboard is the major factor that leads to attainment gains" (2007, 3). They report measurable increases in student achievement in mathematics for both boys and girls who initially scored average or above average on national tests.

Marzano (2009) reports findings from a study that involved eighty-five teachers and 170 classrooms in which the teachers used interactive whiteboards to teach a set of lessons, which they then taught to a different group of students without using the technology. The study results indicated that in general, using interactive whiteboards resulted in a sixteen-percentile-point gain in student achievement.

While statistical data on student achievement associated with the use of an interactive whiteboard is limited, initial findings are encouraging, especially in the area of mathematics.

> **IWB Tips** *from an expert*
>
> The IWB works extremely well for teacher modeling of student tasks with subsequent student interaction. For example, to get students started when working on math problems with manipulatives, a third-grade teacher displayed a digital copy of the activity sheet and manipulatives on the IWB. He modeled two problems on the IWB, with students following along. When it was time for student independent practice, he invited a few students to complete the problems, using manipulatives, on the IWB while the rest continued at their seats. This also provided a nice forum for going over the problems once everyone was finished. Students exhibited more on-task behavior when starting, knowing that they might be chosen to work at the interactive whiteboard.

Changes in Pedagogy

Something less quantifiable in the realm of statistical analysis of student test scores is the overall "sense" that what a teacher does in his or her classroom makes a difference. Research does support the use of highly effective instructional strategies such as small-group guided reading, taking periodic "brain breaks," and providing students with rigorous and relevant instructional tasks. While the actual data supporting the use of interactive whiteboards as a means to improve student achievement is limited, research does show definitively that the use of an IWB as an instructional tool leads to more thoughtful, careful planning and instruction on the part of the teacher (BECTA 2003; Cogill 2008; Glover and Miller 2001). *Pedagogy* refers to the function or work of teaching. It reflects the art, science, or profession of teaching. It encompasses all the best strategies and techniques that the best teachers use every day to optimize student success. The research surrounding the use of IWBs leads one to conclude that the use of an interactive whiteboard is an effective means of reaching more students, keeping them engaged in learning, and providing regular intervals of interaction—all highly effective practices that improve instruction for even the best of teachers.

> *"Interactive whiteboards have great potential as a tool to enhance pedagogical practices in the classroom and ultimately improve student achievement. However, simply assuming that using this or any other technological tool can automatically enhance student achievement would be a mistake. As is the case with all powerful tools, teachers must use interactive whiteboards thoughtfully, in accordance with what we know about good classroom practice."*
>
> —Marzano 2009, 82

Interactive whiteboards have several functions that support and enhance instructional best practices. These include voting tools (used for formative assessments), interactive functions that offer immediate feedback for students, and multimedia options, such as animation and video, that tap into students' different learning modalities.

One sound instructional practice that IWBs support is the use of a student response system (SRS), or voting tool. These "clicker systems" are handheld devices that allow students to respond privately to a projected prompt, question, or problem. The questions can take the form of multiple-choice, yes/no, true/false, and depending on the hardware, short-answer and numerical input. A question is displayed on the screen, and students "click in" their answers using the handheld response device.

> *"After asking a question and getting student responses using voting devices, the teacher should typically discuss the correct answer along with the incorrect answers, making sure to elicit opinions from as many students as possible."*
>
> —Marzano 2009, 82

Since student data are gathered and instantly available to the teacher, an SRS makes it easy to conduct *formative assessment*. Formative assessment has long been a highly effective practice for teachers (Stiggins 2007). Formative assessment is used throughout a unit of study as a means for the teacher to gauge whether students are on track to meet the objectives of the course content before they demonstrate their full understanding on an end-of-unit test or project-based measure. These types of assessments are not intended to be graded; rather, they offer the teacher information about student learning so that the teacher can then support students (or accelerate them) as the learning process continues. The ease of use of the voting system in conjunction with the interactive whiteboard allows teachers to inform instruction regularly and without dramatically interfering with instructional time and instructional routines. In the midst of a lesson, the teacher can ask a question, immediately view student responses, and modify instruction in the moment. Since students can also view class results, they are often more open to further discussion or reteaching by the instructor. Most IWB systems have the voting software integrated, which allows the teacher to stay within a single computer application for instruction, assessment, and reteaching.

> "Both student and teacher must know where the learner is now, how that compares to ultimate learning success, and how to close the gap between the two. Students must not be wondering if they will succeed—only when they will succeed. Obviously, this is the domain of day-to-day classroom assessment."
>
> —Stiggins 2007, 62

Similar to the use of handheld voting devices for immediate feedback is the use of an IWB for interactive practice and games. Graphics, animation, and audible feedback for correct and incorrect responses all contribute to the students' ability to practice basic skills and attend to higher-order thinking tasks when activities are conducted on an interactive whiteboard. For example, students might drag and drop letters in blank spaces (l _ _ p) to make words. If they are correct, they might hear clapping or a bell. If they are wrong, the letter would pop back to its original place. Or, students might make predictions about what will happen during a science investigation and then receive immediate feedback (and an explanation) as to why their prediction was right or wrong. The game-like learning environment that an IWB provides and the immediate feedback keep students interested and motivated to practice more and learn more.

Another improvement in teacher pedagogy with interactive whiteboard use is the idea that teachers can move from one multimedia project or activity to the next with fluidity and purpose. For example, a science teacher introducing changes in Earth's structure might begin by showing a picture of the Grand Canyon or other geological anomaly. After having a class discussion regarding how the land came to look the way it does, the teacher could lead the students directly to an online interactive activity related to changes in the earth and the length of time they take. Afterward, the teacher may have students pair up to discuss what they learned from the interactive game and then write in their science journals to predict how this information applies to the picture of the Grand Canyon. The teacher, using an IWB software function or a simple word-processing program, can record students' ideas to use as a review at the start of science class the next day. All of these activities—the picture viewing, the online game, and the class-written record—can be performed instantly with the use of an IWB. Written work, review work, interactive games and activities, videos, pictures, audio files, and online resources may all be accessed and utilized easily, helping the teacher maintain his or her instructional pace, and thus maximizing the students' instructional time during the school day.

An interactive whiteboard is a must-have for teachers who like to employ active learning strategies in their efforts to improve student achievement. When implemented effectively, an interactive whiteboard allows the teacher to provide engaging tasks for students, monitor the progress of students' skill acquisition easily and frequently, maintain the instructional pace, and develop content smoothly and productively throughout a lesson.

Changes in Student Behavior

One encouraging side effect of the use of interactive whiteboards as documented by both research and anecdotal evidence is the improvement of students' behavior in the classroom. Student-centered learning by nature is more engaging than teacher-centered instruction. Indeed, if students are engaged in their work, they are not engaged in acting out. Miller, Glover, and Averis (2004) noted in their study that use of IWBs shifts instruction from presentation to interaction and students' focus away from teachers and onto content, making interactive whiteboard lessons more student-centered than traditional ones.

Researchers and whiteboard users themselves state how the use of an IWB is a motivational instructional tool, one that captures and maintains the interest of students. Chad Lehman, Media Specialist and Technology Coordinator at Horace Mann Elementary School in West Allis, Wisconsin, noticed a "marked increase in student attentiveness and engagement" since his district began integrating interactive whiteboards into elementary classrooms (Teich 2009, 8th paragraph).

IWB Tips — from an expert

IWBs can have a positive effect on motivation. Kindergarten students sit attentively longer when the teacher is modeling a concept on the IWB or when the students know that they have a turn to use the IWB in front of the class. Students pay attention, are motivated to show what they know or can do using the IWB, and are eager to offer assistance to classmates. Anyone who has taught kindergarten knows how hard it can be to keep the focus of 25 or more five-year-olds for more than just a few minutes!

One cause of student misbehavior is frustration with curriculum content and expectations that are either too challenging or too simple. With an IWB, a teacher can personalize practice problems so that students of all readiness levels have an opportunity to engage in the tasks at the board. For example, when working on double-digit addition problems, the teacher can include problems that require regrouping and others that do not. Knowing the readiness levels of his or her students, the teacher can assign appropriate problems to each student. Likewise, interactive whiteboards allow young students who have not yet mastered fine-motor development to demonstrate their understanding of skills through tapping and dragging objects on the board. This allows students to demonstrate their understanding of a particular skill or concept without the frustration associated with writing. Reduced frustration and increased opportunities for success build students' confidence and keep them motivated to participate in the lesson.

IWB Tips *from an expert*

One kindergarten teacher's favorite IWB activity involves the skill of sequencing. Although many of her students cannot yet effectively communicate their understanding of a story through writing, they can retell the story by sequencing pictures. The students are very excited as they drag the pictures on the IWB into the proper order to show their understanding of the plot. This activity can be modeled with student involvement at the IWB, followed by independent practice with paper pictures at their tables.

> *"Educators can use digital resources while maintaining dynamic interaction with the entire class, provide computer-based learning without isolating students, and encourage a higher level of student interaction in both teacher-directed and group-based exchanges."*
>
> —SMART™ Technologies 2006, 5

The use of an interactive whiteboard is motivating for students. However, McEntyre notes that simply having an interactive whiteboard in and of itself is not motivating; "[r]ather, increased motivation comes from giving students opportunities to interact with the whiteboard" (2006, 4). The use of an interactive whiteboard allows students to manipulate objects; write; type; insert objects, illustrations, and charts; engage in interactive websites; and perform a slew of other tasks, all in an effort to showcase their understanding in front of their peers. This, coupled with the "wow factor" that such an electronic device brings to the classroom, motivates students to pay attention to both the teacher and the students at the board and to participate more regularly in class.

When students are motivated, they attend school more regularly. Students also remain task-focused for longer periods of time, and outbursts and other defiant or disrespectful behaviors decrease. All these effects are directly caused by students being motivated to learn. Since putting IWB technology in the hands of properly trained teachers and staff members, the Jennings School District in St. Louis, Missouri, has noticed improvements in attendance, motivation, and behavior (SMART™ Technologies 2005). If the simple use of an interactive whiteboard is the root of this boost in students' motivation to learn, surely it is an educational tool worth utilizing on a daily basis.

Think About It!

Using an interactive whiteboard can reduce teacher stress by:

- Shortening prep time
- Simplifying resource sharing
- Reaching more students more effectively
- Offering greater flexibility in instructional sequencing and pacing
- Reducing overall anxiety

SMART™ Technologies 2009b

Recap: Using an Interactive Whiteboard

Classroom applications for using interactive whiteboards include:
- Multimedia lessons and presentations including audio and video
- Student- or teacher-centered use
- Collaborative problem solving
- Showcasing student projects and presentations
- Virtual field trips
- Recorded lessons that can be used by substitute teachers
- Formative assessment to immediately inform instruction
- Documentation of student achievement

Teich 2009

Into the Future

The ease of implementation of IWB technology and its integration into teaching practice is certain to increase in the future. Stansbury (2010) notes that new projectors can turn any wall into an IWB. These new projectors can project from short distances, making shadowing nonexistent, and can be adjusted to fit any space, large or small. This technology will be integral to the field of education for the foreseeable future.

Regardless of its make, model, and projection capabilities, an interactive whiteboard is an asset to any teacher's classroom. It helps students make gains in achievement; it helps good teachers engage their students in great lessons; and it turns monotonous work into interactive play, motivating students to want to participate and learn more. This is a wonderful technology tool for teachers!

Chapter Summary

While still relatively new on the education scene, initial research supports the implementation of interactive whiteboards for increased student engagement and achievement. They are also useful instructional tools to support effective teaching practices, and they can save time for teachers. Useful supportive technology, such as interactive software programs and hardware such as student response systems, only add to the overall interactivity of these devices. And, with increased student engagement comes decreased negative student behavior. Researchers have documented evidence to show that effective use of interactive whiteboards benefits the academic and social growth and overall development of students across grade levels and disciplines.

Reflection Questions

1. Think about how research supports the use of an interactive whiteboard in the classroom setting. What do you most look forward to with regard to the use of an IWB?

2. Interactive whiteboards can be used to improve students' learning environment. How do you picture yourself using an IWB with your students? What is your vision?

3. Think back on a lesson you recently taught without the use of an interactive whiteboard. How might the use of an IWB have improved the instructional flow of the lesson, your students' understanding of the concepts or skills, or their level of engagement with the content?

Chapter 2

The Basics of Interactive Whiteboards

This chapter introduces teachers to the five Ws of interactive whiteboard (IWB) technology: the *who, what, where, when,* and *why* of their utilization. The remaining chapters address the *how* of this valuable resource. By the end of this chapter, teachers should be able to reflect on their personal teaching environments and determine why an IWB is an essential piece of instructional technology.

What Are They?

Interactive whiteboards look a lot like the traditional whiteboards found in most classrooms, but they connect to a computer and projector. The computer's desktop is projected onto the whiteboard, where teachers and students can interact with the display. The user can write on the board with a special pen or stylus, and save and print the text on the screen. He or she can touch the board to move objects or perform any number of functions, just like using a computer mouse or touch screen. The user can insert captions, illustrations, clip art, photos, or links to any other instructional media. He or she can complete tables and charts, and insert graphs of the data they enter. In essence, the board does what the user tells it to do.

Many companies produce interactive whiteboards, and the technology advances quickly. The ideas presented in this book reflect the capabilities of IWB technology at the time of publication. Teachers should consider the ideas presented and adapt them to suit the technology available in their current classroom environments. Although teachers may have the most advanced high-tech equipment available to them—or, just the opposite, older IWBs with fewer features—the suggestions for use will help teachers utilize their technology for the ultimate classroom goal: improved instructional practices, increased student engagement, and greater gains in student achievement.

What Are They Not?

Interactive whiteboards are *not* glorified dry-erase boards. Dry-erase boards do not have the capability to interact with the person writing on them; they simply act as a canvas to record a person's words, ideas, or information. Then, with one swift swoop of an eraser, the information is gone. Interactive whiteboards, on the other hand, allow the writer to write or type text and then organize it, embellish it, emphasize it, revise it, edit it, and publish it—or save it, to return to at a later time. Anything that can be done with a computer program can be done on an interactive whiteboard.

Interactive whiteboards are also *not* simply large, bulky screens. Any teacher can project electronic media using a projector and a screen. This particular technology, however, does not allow for interaction with the user. When simply viewing material, students often sit passively absorbing information. They may be held accountable for the content through some form of written assignment or discussion, but the method of delivery does not allow for active, engaging learning opportunities. Interactive classrooms require students to be moving, manipulating, discussing, recording, reflecting, and producing. All these best practices are possible—and easy—with the use of an interactive whiteboard.

Who Uses Them?

> **Lack Height? Sticky Fingers? No Problem!**
>
> If students are not tall enough to reach the top of the IWB with their fingers, use an extension device such as a rubber mallet, a pointer, or an eraser on the tip of a pencil to help students reach high places with confidence and precision. Or keep a small, safety-approved step stool or bench nearby to give students an additional boost.
>
> If sticky or moist fingertips prevent students from dragging items on the board effectively, try a knuckle! A student's knuckle is usually cleaner and drier than a fingertip, and will often work much better. Or, use the eraser on the end of a pencil as a stylus instead.

One of the best features of interactive whiteboards is that students no longer need to be passive listeners and observers in the classroom. Now, they can engage themselves with the lesson, actively participate in class, reflect on their learning, and keep a permanent record of their ideas, all through the use of an interactive whiteboard. Teachers can use them in all classroom settings with students, from one-on-one tutorials to small-group instruction to whole-class demonstrations and lessons. Administrators can use them to conduct professional-development workshops, staff meetings, and presentations for parents. District-level administrators can use them to conduct executive meetings and deliver presentations to the school board or other public forums. Parents can use them during special school assemblies and to conduct PTA meetings. Anyone who projects information for the benefit of others can use an IWB. Interactive whiteboards are an effective presentation tool for any number of people in any number of situations.

Interactive whiteboards need not be reserved just for the classroom. Consider recently aired law-enforcement dramas on television. Investigators use high-tech equipment to pull up case histories, evidence that has been stored electronically, and suspect profiles. They use advanced interactive-whiteboard technology to enlarge, move, sort, and study facts and information relevant to their case. Imagine a classroom environment with entire walls that acted like interactive whiteboards!

Business professionals, too, can benefit from interactive-whiteboard technology. Managers, business leaders, and division representatives can use IWBs when meeting with employees or business teams. An IWB set up in a conference room allows the presenter to move away from dull, one-dimensional slide shows and into more vitalized presentations which include the ability to demonstrate new processes and procedures, show videos, review data, and record ideas. According to IBC Systems, SMART™ Technologies offers business-minded hardware and software especially suited to "bring everyone into one room—regardless of location—to share ideas, work on documents, and focus efforts on common goals" (2011, under Business Solutions). They have information specific to a wide range of businesses, from architecture, engineering, and construction to telecommunications.

As much as businesses can benefit from interactive-whiteboard technology, so too can community organizations. Community leaders meet with organizational teams, conduct public forums, or make presentations to elected officials.

Some IWB manufacturers also provide specific hardware and software solutions for those who work in government settings. They offer ideas and methods for interactive presentations, distance collaboration, and effective training. These apply to government workers in general, military personnel, and public safety officials.

In fact, anyone who shares or discusses information with small groups of people can improve his or her presentation by using an interactive whiteboard.

> **Recap: People Who Use Interactive Whiteboards**
>
> Interactive whiteboards are beneficial devices for:
> - Teachers
> - College professors
> - Administrators
> - Professional-development presenters
> - Students
> - Parents
> - Business leaders
> - Community leaders
> - Government workers

Where Are They Most Useful?

Interactive whiteboards are useful teaching devices. However, like all devices, they have their limitations. Interactive whiteboards are most useful in small spaces, such as a classroom or a conference room. They would not be suitable for whole-school assemblies in gymnasiums or during large-scale presentations in an auditorium. Interactive whiteboards measure about the size of a standard classroom projector screen. Most auditoriums have projection systems that are much larger than this. So, a whiteboard system would be too small in this type of setting.

Besides the general education classroom, an IWB can serve teachers and students in many other locations around a school building. A media specialist can use IWB technology in the media center to teach students about multimedia tools, research skills, or any other media-related topics.

IWB Tips *from an expert*

Media specialists often use their IWBs when working with students on research skills. Using the simple annotation capabilities of the IWB over nonfiction text (from a Web page, a PDF file, or a digital textbook), they can highlight, circle, or underline headings, pertinent facts, or supporting details. They can then switch from the nonfiction text to a blank screen and model how to take notes on the information presented. Inviting volunteers to the IWB to demonstrate their knowledge is very engaging for the students!

Technology teachers, of course, can use IWB technology in their instructional setting for modeling or practicing usage of search engines, software applications, or technology features of published curriculum. Special education or Title I resource classrooms especially benefit from the use of IWB technology. Typically, these students benefit from multimodal, interactive, and engaging instruction. The use of an IWB is an effective instructional tool to help reach these specific learners and their individual needs. (For information on how to use an IWB to differentiate instruction, see Chapter 7.)

IWB Tips *from an expert*

Our resource teachers work with special-needs students and use their IWBs to engage students in ways not possible without the technology. One lead resource teacher emphatically stated, "Before we had our IWB, I had three students who would not attend to an instructional setting under any circumstance. When we started to use the IWB (using pictures of the students in the class for various sorting activities), those three students enthusiastically participated and later showed transfer of the concepts! They'll now go to the board on their own—even when the projector is off!"

Administrators might want to install an IWB in a conference room for use during workshops or meetings. A music teacher could use an interactive whiteboard in a music room to engage his or her students more fully in lessons. Any setting in which instructors or presenters want learners or audience members to actively engage in their lessons or presentations is a good place for an interactive whiteboard.

Did You Know?

A solar-powered interactive whiteboard is bringing this instructional technology to students in a part of Africa where there is little electricity.

PR Newswire 2011

When Should They Be Used?

Think about the number of transitions that occur within a single lesson. Consider the following situation: Mrs. Hill is a highly effective teacher. She uses multiple approaches to reach students of all readiness levels during her mathematics instruction. She is adept at managing her lessons. She is concise and precise in her teaching. She strategically utilizes various instructional tools such as manipulatives, interactive software, and individual student dry-erase boards to introduce, teach, practice, and evaluate students' success with content. Unfortunately, Mrs. Hill loses valuable instructional time moving from one tool to the next. First, she introduces the class to a new topic with a short video clip that she streams from the Internet. This requires her projector and screen, which covers her board. She must also run the video from behind her desk, where her computer must remain in order for it to connect to the projector. She believes in illustrating ideas with real-world applications such as the one on the video, but she dislikes feeling so isolated from her class. She is not a "behind-the-desk" kind of teacher.

Once the movie is done, Mrs. Hill adjusts the setting on her projector to read her document camera. She hands out the student manipulatives, regains everyone's attention, and then demonstrates the concept from the video with hands-on experiences. Again, Mrs. Hill likes modeling what students' materials should look like using the manipulatives under the document camera, but she is still separated from her students since the document camera, too, is beside her desk. Once the class has practiced the concept using manipulatives, they move to abstract problems. For this, Mrs. Hill must roll up her screen and turn off her projector. The students put their manipulatives away and pull out their individual whiteboards. As Mrs. Hill demonstrates how to work through problems on the board, the students practice at their seats with their individual whiteboards. When they turn their boards toward Mrs. Hill, she can check students' understanding of the concept.

Next, students take out their math textbooks. The students who are not clear on the procedures gather together around Mrs. Hill's work table. While others in the class work independently, Mrs. Hill conducts a small-group lesson, using a portable chart-paper stand and markers to demonstrate the concept further as the students around her work in their books.

How many transitions take place in the scene described above? They involve computer, document camera, whiteboard, desk work, and small groups. Every time Mrs. Hill moves from one task to the next, she loses instructional time in the transition. Also, she was physically distanced from her students for much of the lesson. She could not easily oversee her students' independent work because she had to run her instruction from behind her computer and document camera. These routines could be more smoothly connected if Mrs. Hill had an interactive whiteboard in her classroom. With an IWB, she could run the video, open an online manipulative website (which the students also could manipulate at the board), write on an IWB blank page, and pull up an electronic version of the math text to model procedures. Additionally, Mrs. Hill could gather her small group around the IWB and use it to teach her follow-up lesson. Mrs. Hill's dynamic lesson would be that much more effective were she to utilize interactive-whiteboard technology. She would have the benefit of being close to the students, and she would have the option of calling on students to demonstrate processes—a much more engaging instructional strategy than simply showing projected images.

Imagine the fluidity of an entire day following the structure an IWB provides in the classroom. This example shares one lesson on one day in one mathematics class. But, the idea holds true for any instructional setting in any subject area at any time during the school day.

IWB Tips *from an expert*

Although it required some preparation time up front, a third-grade teacher placed all the student math pages (provided in PDF format by the publisher) in the IWB software (in this case, SMART Notebook™) for use in his math lessons for the whole year. This allowed him and his students to use the IWB throughout entire math lessons. From instruction to modeling to guided and then independent practice, the teacher and students interacted with the IWB, which brought increased engagement and understanding to the lesson.

Why Should They Be Used?

Interactive whiteboards offer much more than traditional whiteboards. Writing (or word processing) is not the only action they can perform; IWBs are a valuable instructional tool that allows the teacher to instruct and monitor students without being locked behind a piece of furniture. They allow students to maintain a high level of engagement with the teacher and therefore the content. The teacher and his or her students can both be up and moving, acting as integral participants in the lesson rather than passive learners. Interactive whiteboards keep the teacher (or more importantly, the students) at center stage, with the focus on content and process with few interruptions as a lesson moves fluidly from one task to the next.

> **From the Trenches**
>
> *"I discovered I have very little need now for my document camera. When I want to do simple math practice problems with the class, I open a word processing program, then use the pen tools to write on the interactive whiteboard. My IWB makes practice so easy. And, I am not stuck beside my document camera to demonstrate mathematical processes."*
>
> —Tabetha Harrison,
> Third-Grade Teacher

Likewise, students with varied learning styles require different types of instructional strategies. For instance, students who are kinesthetic learners benefit greatly from being able to actively touch and manipulate the items projected on the board. Kinesthetic learners learn best by doing, experiencing, touching, moving, or being active in some way. Jensen (2008) links physical activity to positive effects on the brain, and suggests that teachers plan activities that have a built-in component of physical movement. The use of an IWB naturally provides for active learning. Students with poor fine-motor coordination may feel empowered and confident as they use gross-motor skills to interact with the board. Teachers frequently utilize text and pictures, models, projection screens, computers, film and video, multi-image media, color highlighting, organizing information, imagery, and graphic organizers to stimulate reasoning and learning for students with disabilities. Logsdon reminds us that "[m]ost students, with a disability or not, enjoy the engaging variety that multisensory techniques can offer" (accessed 2011). The use of an interactive whiteboard provides teachers with meaningful, relevant, and engaging work that benefits their students with disabilities as well as their general education students.

Consider this science situation: In a traditional classroom, students learn from a lesson in their textbook. They read factual information, using pictures and other visuals and their captions to support the content. The teacher asks questions, and the students answer them. After reading about the content, students complete a graphic organizer to summarize the information and then answer comprehension questions. If a teacher uses electronic media to present information, he or she does so from one computer, to which the students generally do not have access. So, the teacher winds up being the one to manipulate or demonstrate the projected images. In a classroom with an interactive whiteboard, however, the lesson becomes much more active. The teacher can project the text on the screen and invite students to circle, underline, or highlight the important information, which the students can then use immediately to complete the graphic organizer. Or, the teacher can pull up a digital copy of the graphic organizer and toggle between the text and worksheet to model how to find and record important information. The students, although not using the board themselves, have an immediate visual that they can use to continue working independently. Or, the teacher can hand over the highlighter to the students, and they can, in turn, come to the board to show the class where the most important information is on the page. When the teacher pulls up an electronic interactive activity, the students can be the ones to move, sort, tap, and "play," instead of the teacher. Additionally, after the teacher is done modeling the graphic organizer on the IWB and directs the students to complete their paper versions at their desks, he or she can invite a pair of students to finish their graphic organizer on the IWB. In this situation, the IWB transforms a science lesson from a "sit and get" to an interactive, engaging learning process in which the students "run the show" with the teacher's guidance.

Finally, the use of an interactive whiteboard engages learners through activity, interaction, and, most importantly, immediate feedback. Brookhart describes effective feedback as that which "contains information students can use." For example, when learning basic facts or simple skills (such as identifying nouns or sequencing events), students "need immediate information about whether an answer is right or wrong" (2008, 55). Interaction with an IWB provides the instant feedback students need to learn new skills.

Recap: Why Use an Interactive Whiteboard?
- Present instructional material more fluidly
- Maintain proximity to students
- Offer students ready access to large-scale, interactive instructional programs and manipulatives
- Provide immediate feedback for students
- Improve students' focus on lesson content

Chapter Summary

This chapter should have teachers excited about using interactive-whiteboard technology with their students. If anyone is new to the IWB community, welcome! This technology is proven to bring engaging learning to students. For veteran IWB users looking for new ideas to refresh and revitalize their use of an IWB, the next chapters should offer some innovative ideas.

Reflection Questions

1. After reading about the *who*, *what*, *where*, *when*, and *why* of IWBs, how do you see an interactive whiteboard in your classroom benefiting both your lesson presentation and the students you teach?

2. Think about a student in your class who needs specialized instructional strategies to help him or her learn. How can the use of an IWB support his or her learning, as well as enhance the learning of other students in your classroom?

Chapter 3

Interactive Whiteboards in the Classroom

Often, when new programs, instructional resources, or teaching techniques come along—which happens quite frequently in education—teachers have questions about how to go about integrating the new material and ideas. Some teachers jump in with both feet, trusting that they will be able to troubleshoot glitches and bumps along the way when they encounter them. Some teachers are much more reserved about implementing new ideas; they might try one new idea here or there until their confidence grows and then fully embrace the new resources. Yet other teachers resist new ideas and approaches to teaching and learning—they need repeated trainings, continuous encouragement, and active modeling or coaching before they feel comfortable enough to take the reins and apply their new learning or resource on their own. Regardless of a teacher's approach to new techniques, interactive-whiteboard technology offers a great opportunity to experiment with or refine instructional practices.

Administrators and colleagues want their teachers and peers to be successful with whatever strategies and materials they utilize in their efforts to improve student achievement. Professional educators know that no program, tool, or technique is perfect. This is also true of interactive whiteboards. However, the ideas in this book should help teachers wade through the murky waters and use the technology to its utmost potential. This chapter addresses questions teachers may have with regard to successful implementation of the use of IWBs.

Classroom Organization

Teachers manage countless people, places, and things throughout the school day. They make organizational decisions such as placement of student desks, tables, bookcases, and other furniture and resources such as word walls and bulletin boards. They organize whole-group instruction, small-group instruction, peer collaboration, and individual reviews and conferences as part of an instructional plan. They gather material resources such as books, flip charts, and handouts; consumable supplies such as pencils and paper; equipment such as science tools, math manipulatives, clipboards, scissors, and staplers; and a host of other gadgets and products necessary to transition from one subject or class period to the next. Yes, a teacher's day is busy with organizing supplies and materials to help instruction run smoothly. When a teacher adds an interactive whiteboard to the list of supplies to manage, careful planning with regard to the *where* will help a teacher pull off the *how* with reduced effort.

One consideration with regard to the classroom management of an interactive whiteboard is the placement of the board in the classroom. This will drive other organizational strategies such as who will use it, when it will be used within a lesson, and how often it will be used throughout the day. Most teachers place their interactive whiteboard in the center at the front of their room. If the school or district has installed ceiling-mounted projectors, this decision will have been pretty much made for them; the board goes where the projector shines. Leave space in front of the board for everyone to access it easily. If it is a freestanding board (meaning that it is portable and not wall-mounted), teachers might want to place boxes or bookcases on either side of it to minimize movement. Although one tip to successful IWB implementation is the reorienting of the board each time it is used, the boxes on either side of it will help keep people from tripping over the legs that protrude out in front of the board (see Figure 3.1).

Figure 3.1 Box Placement Under Portable Interactive Whiteboard

Also, for teachers who are in the routine of calling students up to the front of the room for whole- or small-group instruction, this will leave space for them to continue to do so. In intermediate classrooms, be sure students can turn to face the board easily. Figures 3.2 and 3.3 show how primary and secondary classrooms might be set up with the interactive whiteboard taking center stage at the front of the room. While in most classrooms the IWB is indeed located at the front of the room, consideration must also be given to traditional whiteboard space and location. If a classroom is outfitted with an interactive whiteboard, retention of a regular whiteboard is critical for written information that students might need to reference even when the projector is turned off.

Figure 3.2 Sample Primary Classroom Layout

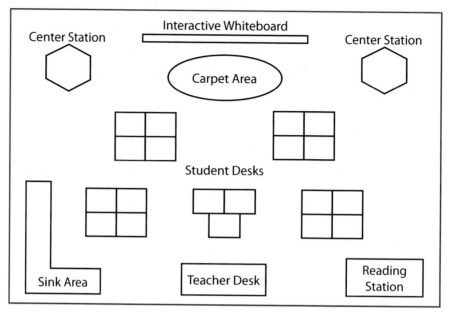

Figure 3.3 Sample Secondary Classroom Layout

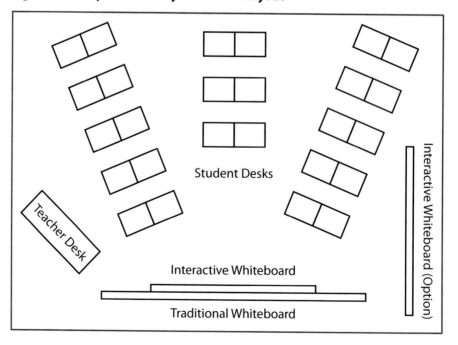

Besides classroom placement, teachers should also consider the height of the board. The top of the board should be easily reached by the smallest users yet be tall enough for students to see when seated at their desks. Since the purpose of an IWB is for students to interact with the projected information and images, this board may rest in a lower position than would a traditional dry-erase whiteboard. Students should feel successful and proud of their work and not frustrated that they cannot demonstrate understanding simply because a picture, a blank line, or a software menu is out of reach. One way to correct for an IWB that is mounted a bit high for young users is to merely use the zoom on the projector to make the image smaller on the IWB. If the bottom of the projected image is then aimed at the bottom of the IWB, the top of the projected image is below the top of the board. There is no rule that says the projected image needs to fill the entire board!

Once teachers determine the position and optimal height of the IWB, they can set their projector to shine directly on the board. Teachers should consider the projector's *throw ratio*—a measure that compares the distance of the projector from the screen to the size of the projected image. If the projector is placed too far from the IWB, the projected image might be larger than the board; and if the projector is placed too close to the board, the projected image will be too small. Position the projector far enough away from the board to optimize the IWB's board space, but not so far away that the image overlaps the edges of the board. If too many computer features project outside the borders of the IWB, neither the teacher nor the students will be able to access the information they may need on the touch screen. Most projectors also have a "keystone" adjustment, which allows the user to adjust the image so that the sides of the projected image are parallel to the edges of the IWB.

The placement of the interactive whiteboard in the classroom is mostly up to teacher preference. However, it should also support the purpose of the IWB for a majority of the instructional time. Some teachers have found success with the board in the back of the room. Others argue that this placement does not commit the teacher to using the technology throughout the day since the traditional board still takes center stage in the classroom, thus encouraging traditional instruction. The information in Figure 3.4 lists some advantages and disadvantages to setting up an IWB in different locations around the classroom. If possible, teachers may want to try different locations to see which works best for them and their students.

Figure 3.4 Classroom Organizational Strategies for IWB Placement

Placement	Advantages	Disadvantages
Front of Room	• Full access by students • Central for whole-class instruction • Commits teacher to accept and utilize up-to-date technology or change pedagogy	• Need to leave space for whole-class work at the front of room • If portable, it is easily bumped or tripped over • Lose most or all traditional board space
Back of Room	• Adds a second lesson area • More easily used as a learning center for small-group and individual work • Keeps traditional board space at the front of the room for listing class messages, essential questions, routines, schedules, or other all-day posts	• Students may have to turn away from their desks for whole-class lessons • Does not commit teacher to accept and utilize up-to-date technology or change pedagogy
Side Wall or Corner	• Portable installation means it can be moved to meet varied classroom organizational needs, or it can be shared among classrooms • Great for small-group work or center activities	• Not the most strategic position for consistent use • May block access to counters, bulletin boards, cabinets, or bookcases

Classroom Management

Now that the whiteboard is installed and functioning, it is time to think about how the use of this board will mesh with the overall classroom structure and routines. Having set up the IWB in the most suitable location will help eliminate some classroom management issues that might arise. Classroom management includes time management, materials organization, student organization, task appropriateness, motivation, and a consistent discipline system. Since research has shown that regular use of an IWB increases engagement and motivation, thus reducing behavior issues (see Chapter 1), suggestions for discipline are not addressed in this section. The only advice to offer is this: Teachers should use their board as often as possible, and they should allow students to regularly engage with the content through the use of the board.

As illustrated in Chapter 2, the use of an IWB can improve time management in the classroom. Instead of spending precious instructional time sorting through countless teacher's guides and student handouts or transitioning from computer to whiteboard to document camera, all of a lesson's resources can be pulled up and ready to go with the simple touch of the screen. Especially with textbook publishers moving to digital formats and the ready availability of myriad books, practice activities, videos, and other electronic media, IWBs are an effective means through which to store and access all of these digital resources. For example, a teacher can engage students with an interactive online activity (e.g., sorting words with *r*-controlled vowels). Then, he or she can read an eBook on the IWB. As students read, they can highlight all the words with *r*-controlled vowels to reinforce this decoding skill. Then, the teacher can provide a hard copy of a storyboard graphic organizer, which can also be displayed on the IWB. The teacher can guide the students in beginning the organizer, then students can continue in small collaborative learning groups or independently. At the end of the lesson, students can share their completed storyboards with the whole class as the teacher records the information in the digital version on the IWB. This self-checking system provides immediate feedback for students. Finally, the class can round out the lesson by free-writing words with *r*-controlled vowels in a word-processing program, also on the IWB. This list can be printed and posted for the teacher and students to reference as their study of decoding *r*-controlled vowels continues in future lessons.

All the materials listed in the scenario above (e.g., the online activity, the eBook, the graphic organizer, and the word-processing document) can be pulled up by the teacher prior to the lesson and minimized on the computer's desktop. Then, when the teacher moves from one activity to the next, he or she can open the needed resource by simply touching the screen. Or, each electronic resource may be digitally linked to one or two IWB lesson pages and accessed directly from the IWB slides (see Chapter 6 for information on how to link pages). This minimizes downtime in between activities, and it keeps the teacher fully engaged with his or her class throughout the entire lesson. Also, while some students are at the board, the teacher can monitor those who remain at their desks, offering additional instructional support as needed. The use of the IWB helps the teacher with all aspects of classroom management: time, task appropriateness, materials, and engagement.

As with any new instructional tool, teachers should not feel compelled to master every aspect all at once. Having goals that are too lofty will leave teachers feeling disappointed, frustrated, and overwhelmed. These feelings will inevitably lead to implementation failure or, at the very least, minimized usage. Start small. Focus on one subject area, and find or develop interactive lessons to support instruction. Build a personal repertoire as the school year progresses. Strive to learn just one or two new "tricks" each week. Build an IWB skill set gradually. If a lesson does not go as envisioned, evaluate what went wrong. Attempt to correct the shortcomings another day. Do not expect everything to go perfectly every time the board is in use.

> **IWB Tips** *from an expert*
>
> For teachers new to the technology, one great way to "start small" is to utilize interactive websites on the board. This is a comfortable and pedagogically sound place to start, as it allows for an authentic and engaging use of the IWB without having to create activities or even maneuver within the IWB software. I often see teachers using two wonderful math manipulative websites on their IWBs: http://nlvm.usu.edu and http://illuminations.nctm.org. These two sites offer numerous interactive opportunities to support almost any mathematics topic. Although some may view this type of IWB use as lower on the technology-integration curve since the activity is not teacher-created, it is an engaging, developmentally appropriate, kinesthetic use of the tool.

Classroom management also refers to the teacher's ability to effectively transition groups of students as they move from one location in the room to another and to set clear expectations with regard to guided and independent practice. Students who understand the tasks set before them more readily attend to them, and they require less redirection while the teacher is engaged with other students. Consider the use of an interactive whiteboard as a classroom-management assistant. The board can be used to facilitate small-group instruction while other students are engaged in an independent activity, or it can be used as a center activity for a small group of students while the teacher is engaged in a direct instruction with other students. For example, during a differentiated math block, the teacher might pull a small group of students together near the IWB to review a specific skill using online manipulatives or to play an interactive game. This allows the teacher to direct the activity rather than have students independently practice these skills with the interactive programs. So, the teacher guides the practice and gives immediate feedback about student success with the skill. Or, while students work independently to complete an activity sheet, a small group of students can work collaboratively at the IWB to play a math game related to a specific skill or engage in an enrichment online math activity to supplement and extend their learning. This allows the teacher time to work with individuals or small groups of students to review their independent practice and provide more individualized feedback with regard to the math skill.

IWB Tips *from an expert*

In first-grade classrooms, teachers have groups of two or three students using the IWB engaged in simple word work activities during the literacy block. The students are able to work independently because the teacher has introduced the vocabulary activity to the whole group at an earlier time. These vocabulary activities include interactive websites (such as the primary site http://www.Starfall.com), simple teacher-created drag-and-drop sorting activities, and erase-to-reveal exercises. Other students in the class are engaged in meaningful traditional activities while the teacher is conferencing or goal-setting with individual students. In this scenario, the IWB is a meaningful activity station added to the existing repertoire of independent choices for students.

Great Idea!

Teachers can create self-checking activities on the interactive whiteboard. These are great for small-group workstations. There are many ways to do this. The IWB software likely has built-in activities or graphic options that allow for self-checking. Teachers can type an answer and then paint or scribble over it. When students respond, they check their answer by erasing the paint or markings. Another option is to place a solid figure over the text. To self-check, students simply move the figure away to uncover the answer. Try different techniques to see which one works best to keep students interested in the "big reveal." For ready-made activities, teachers can search online using any of the websites listed in Appendix C, or conduct a search for themselves.

Other Classroom Management Tips

The following ideas can help teachers use their interactive whiteboards to assist with classroom management:

- Assign one student to be the aligner or orienteer as a classroom job. This person has the responsibility to orient the board before class begins and throughout the day as needed.

- Complete lesson plans in advance using electronic media. Embed or link URLs, PDFs, other word-processing documents, or any other electronic resources to the lesson plan document. Pull up the one lesson plan and have access to all of the instructional tools from one convenient location.

- Use the recording tool to record a lesson. Play it back for absent students the following day. Or teachers can simply use it as a review lesson on a day when they are absent. (Easy substitute plans!) This idea is explored more fully in Chapter 6.

- Use the interactive tools to every advantage. Keep students interested and engaged by selecting a different pen design or highlighter color for different purposes. Reward good behavior by having students who are most engaged make the design and color selections.

- Use colleagues, blogs, and support resources to every advantage. Ask questions, seek answers, and adapt others' suggestions to suit the classroom's needs.

Classroom Tip!

Teachers can install a wireless mouse on their classroom computer. For IWB functions that are best used directly from the computer, students can still interact with the activity. Place the mouse on their desk, and let them click and drag to show what they know!

Maintenance

The interactive whiteboard will need regular cleaning to keep it properly maintained. Fortunately, this process is quick and simple for the user. Regular maintenance on an interactive whiteboard requires three tools: a lint-free cloth, high-quality glass cleaner, and canned air.

For light board cleanings, spray a small amount of high-quality glass cleaner on the lint-free cloth. Wipe the board down as you would any other major appliance or electronic equipment. In the case of a SMART™ brand interactive whiteboard, if the penlights do not illuminate when the pens are removed from the tray, try blowing air from an air can all around the pen tray. This should loosen and remove any dust particles that may be interfering with the pen and tray connection.

Most projectors have a simple filter that should be cleaned on a monthly or bimonthly basis. Refer to the owner's manual on how to remove the filter, which is easily blown clear of lint and then reinstalled. In almost all projectors, this is a user-serviceable item. For more involved maintenance, contact the school or district's information-technology specialist. Maintaining an interactive whiteboard is just as easy as maintaining a computer or any other electrical equipment for which teachers may be responsible.

> **Uh-oh!**
>
> Did someone write on the IWB with permanent marker? Don't fret just yet! Try marking over the marks with a dry-erase marker and then wiping it clean. Repeat this process as needed to remove all traces of the permanent marker.

Software Updates

Electronic software generally needs periodic updating. This is because the makers of software are continuously modifying, upgrading, and improving their technology. Usually, these updates come free with software purchases. This should be true of the interactive-whiteboard software that came with the board in the classroom. Most of the time, these software updates are easily checked and the installation is as simple as clicking the mouse. To check for software updates for the interactive whiteboard, find the function that allows for this. If it is not easy to identify on the whiteboard software, a teacher can search online or via the *help* option contained within the software program. The help option is usually placed at the top of the software toolbar. Then, teachers should follow the prompts to install the most current version of the software. If no updates are necessary, a dialogue box will indicate this, and the teacher can exit out of the "check for updates" option.

Troubleshooting

Nothing is more frustrating than having a dynamite lesson or activity sidelined by a glitch in technology. However, teachers should try not to get too frustrated with technology hiccups. Troubleshooting the system is often an effective solution. The glitch might be something as simple as a loose cord. These helpful tips might help a user make amends with his or her IWB.

> **Remember!**
>
> Technology is only as good as its technology support system. Get to know the information technology (IT) professional at your school well. Smile and be understanding. Say *thank you*, even if the problem is not resolved when you would like it to be.

Problem Area 1: Blank Screen, or Unresponsive or Missing "Ready" Light

Check: Power supplies, cables, connections, and cords. Be sure everything is plugged in correctly and that the connections are tight and secure. Be sure the computer, projector, and IWB are all turned on. Try rebooting the computer and/or restarting the IWB. Also, try unplugging all the connections and then reconnecting them. Turn off the computer and then reconnect the IWB cord. If the board is still unresponsive, try attaching the computer to another board. If the new board works, the former board may be in need of repairs. If the new board does not work, there may be an issue with the computer itself. One option to consider is a reinstallation of the IWB software. You might have to contact the technology professional to investigate the problem.

Problem Area 2: Blinking, Darkness, or Dark Images

Check: Projector. The projector is a natural dust collector. Environmental conditions, too, play a role in its ability to function effectively. It may need a new filter, or the filter may need a good cleaning. In some cases, the bulb may need to be replaced. The IT professional can show teachers how to clean projector filters and replace bulbs. It is a good idea not to attempt to clean or replace anything on the projector without approval.

Problem Area 3: Misplaced Taps

Check: Calibration or orientation of the board. It is always a good idea to recalibrate or reorient the screen at the start of each day and periodically throughout the day (e.g., at the start of each lesson). The orientation or calibration is a process in which the projected image is "aligned" with the IWB so when the user touches the IWB, the touch is registered in the correct place on the projected image. It is immediately obvious if the IWB is not correctly calibrated because when the board is touched in one spot, the touch is registered in a different place on the projected image. A board that is mounted on a moveable stand will most likely need to be recalibrated more often than a mounted board. This is also true if the projector is on a cart rather than ceiling-mounted.

Problem Area 4 (boards with styli only): Unresponsive Styli

Check: Marker trays. Try blowing out dust in the trays with canned air. Then, the system may need to be restarted to get everything functioning as one unit. (See the tips from Problem Area 1.)

Join Other Professionals!

Teachers who like to blog may consider joining *The Interactive Whiteboard Revolution.* Bloggers post successes, challenges, and opinions about everything related to interactive whiteboards on this website: http://iwbrevolution.ning.com.

Problem Area 5 (boards with styli only): Overactive Styli

Check: Tools option. Be sure to have the pointer tool selected. Place all four pens and the eraser in their proper places. Be sure the IWB is not reading one as being active (as indicated by a lighted tray). If this happens, try blowing dust from the pen tray with canned air. If using a pen stylus, be sure to have the proper writing tool selected. Teachers can check and adjust the style of the writing tool by choosing the Pen option and opening the Pen tools (right-click). Select the color and thickness of choice (See Figure 3.5).

Figure 3.5 Line Style Menu

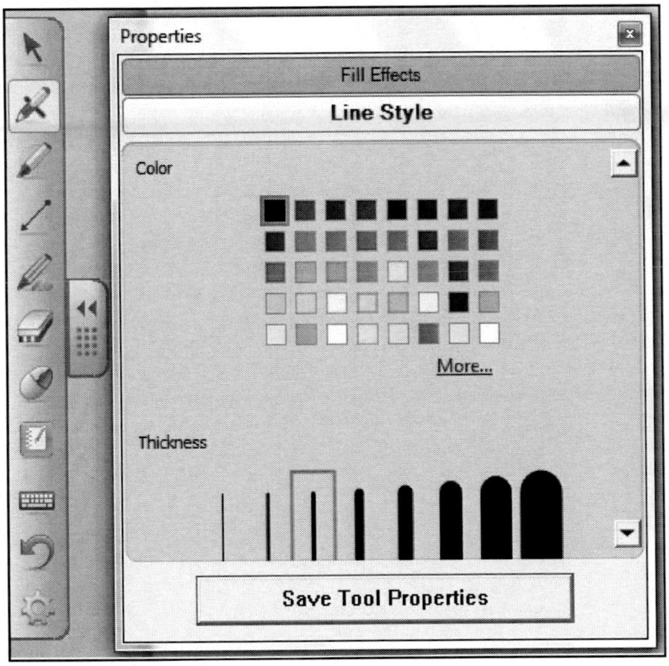

Problem Area 6: No Sound

Check: Speaker connections and computer's mute system. Be sure the speakers are plugged into the correct port on the computer (see Figure 3.6). Teachers with a classroom sound system should be sure it has been turned on. Try turning off the entire system, then starting it again. Or, if using computer speakers, be sure they are turned on. This is usually indicated by a green light on one or both of the speakers. Check the computer's sound options. Make sure the mute option is not checked. (Muted sound is shown in Figure 3.7.) Also, be sure the volume is raised.

Figure 3.6 Headphone Port

Figure 3.7 Volume Control

IWB Tips from an expert

We often underestimate the potential impact of what we do in our classrooms. A fourth-grade teacher created a relatively simple IWB file that allowed the students to drag their names into a matrix that identified the part of the writing process in which they were engaged. The teacher at any point during writing time could glance up at the IWB and immediately see where any student was in the writing process. Students would drag their name to a new spot as they moved to the next stage of their writing. I encouraged this teacher to share her idea at a staff meeting, but her initial reply was "But it's so simple. I don't think anyone will benefit." However, within a week of sharing at the staff meeting, I walked into a second-grade classroom and observed the teacher using an iteration of the original fourth-grade IWB file to track student choice for center time. The second-grade teacher, after the staff meeting, had asked the fourth-grade teacher for her file and then modified it for her use. Ask your colleagues about how they use their IWBs, and don't underestimate your great ideas!

Chapter Summary

This chapter identified key issues related to effective and efficient interactive whiteboard use in the classroom.

Teachers can be their own best support group. Stop by one another's rooms to chat about a great lesson or share a newly found IWB function. Start a blog on a school or district website so teachers can interact with each other electronically. YouTube™ has ready-access to a plethora of interactive whiteboard videos in a wide range of topics—from management and maintenance to beginning and advanced features, to fun and engaging lessons.

Reflection Questions

1. What challenges are most concerning to you with regard to the use of an IWB in your classroom? How can the ideas or suggestions in this chapter help you overcome these challenges?

2. What additional resources can you refer to with questions regarding classroom organization, classroom management, or IWB maintenance? Where can you find support? Create a list of resources and a brief summary of how each resource can provide support.

Chapter 4

Designing Effective Lessons with Interactive-Whiteboard Technology

IWB 101

An interactive whiteboard is an instructional tool that teachers can use to maximize learning while simultaneously minimizing downtime, disruptive behavior, and teacher stress. After learning about the whys and hows of using interactive whiteboards in the classroom, the next step is to plug it in and give it a run. Teachers may jump right in and develop a lesson of their own using the IWB software. They may access a game, an informational page, or an activity on the Internet to project onto the IWB. Another first step may be to download and try one or more ready-made IWB lessons from the Internet. Exploring and sampling lessons and activities with the IWB is a sure way to discover something new, energize teaching, and improve student engagement. For a quick how-to guide for navigating SMART Notebook™ software, see Appendix A. Appendix B offers guidelines for using ActivInspire™ software.

> **Teacher Tip!**
>
> Teachers can practice using the IWB software on their computers without it being connected to the board. This way, teachers can explore the IWB software features and design and develop engaging and effective lesson plans and lesson pages whenever and wherever is most convenient for them.

While exploring and sampling interactive-whiteboard software and activities is a great way to familiarize oneself with this new technology, teachers will eventually want to use their IWB in a more strategic fashion to optimize learning in the classroom. This chapter moves into learning strategies for using an interactive whiteboard to support and enhance instructional lesson planning. Every credentialed teacher has learned how to write an effective lesson plan. As an instructional tool, the use of an interactive whiteboard falls right into place throughout all stages of an effective lesson plan. This chapter shares ideas on how to use an IWB as an integral part of the lesson routine.

Figure 4.1 Lesson Plan Model Aligned to IWB Use

Lesson Segment	Description	IWB Integration
Objectives/ Standards	Sets the purpose for the lesson; drives the lesson plan development for the teacher, and sets clear outcomes for students	Use a pull tab to list essential questions and to focus or review questions or lesson objectives.
Anticipatory Set	"The Hook"; piques students' interest; gets students personally involved and interested in the content; assesses prior knowledge	• Access an online media file, picture, or document to view and discuss • Pose a question and write freely to answer it • Complete a class K-W-L chart • Conduct a short, engaging prelearning activity
Input Modeling: Checking for Understanding	The teacher teaches and demonstrates ideas; builds students' understanding of a concept or skill; allows students to "see how it works" before trying it themselves	• Use interactive activities and programs • Use eBooks, projectable books, or other electronic reading media • Use interactive math manipulatives • Show videos • Play interactive games • Conduct an online simulation activity
Guided Practice	Allows students to communicate what they have learned so far with teacher direction and support	
Closure	"The Wrap-Up"; teacher and students review and summarize what they learned	Use a pull tab to review essential questions and to focus or review questions or lesson objectives
Independent Practice	Demonstration of student learning with little, if any, teacher direction	• Post assignments, including textbook pages, prompts, and project summaries • Project graphic organizers for students to complete independently following a reading selection or learning experience • Project a literacy-center schedule or learning-extension ideas

Adapted from Madeline Hunter (1982)

Writing Lesson Plans for the IWB

Imagine a day when the teacher walks into the classroom, projects one image, and the rest of the day flows smoothly from one concept to the next. The steps of a lesson transition naturally from beginning to end. The teacher meets all of the intended objectives. And the students are engaged, and the teacher has evidence of their learning. The use of interactive technology can bring any teacher to this level of engagement in the classroom. Will it happen on the first day? Probably not. Over time, teachers will develop a repertoire of highly effective, highly engaging IWB lessons. They will need to begin by focusing their attention on one subject area, one major concept, or one major lesson plan component as they improve their personal IWB skill set and begin to utilize the advanced features that are available. Teachers should not expect everything to run flawlessly the first time they launch a full lesson using the IWB. A good day in today's classroom is a day without any technology glitches. Given the necessary reliance on persnickety wiring, hardware, and software, teachers should expect to be frustrated at times as they move forward full throttle with the available technology.

So, how can teachers begin to develop lessons for their interactive whiteboards? All IWBs come with software that allows teachers to bring curriculum content to the board. Two popular examples of this type of software are SMART's Notebook™ software and Promethean's ActivInspire™ software. Although the different brands of IWBs come with different software, the functionality is the same—they give the user a canvas for curriculum content. The teacher has the choice of creating content from scratch or utilizing any of the thousands of pre-created lessons in the software. After reading this chapter about how an IWB can support all facets of lesson plan development, open a blank page in the program and begin developing ideas. As suggested, start small. Only get as complex as a personal comfort level will allow. There will always be time to get fancy as the IWB software becomes more familiar.

Teachers who have ready-made slide show presentations for particular lessons are in luck! The IWB software should allow them to open, project, and utilize what they already have prepared. Presentation tools appear on the screen so that teachers may stand at the IWB to run the presentation. They can change slides, mark up the presentation with notes or drawings using the pens from the tray, and then choose to save or not save the mark-ups. Saved drawings and writing will become permanent parts of the slide show.

Likewise, for teachers who have lesson plans already completed using a word-processing program, these, too, will interface with the IWB. Simply open the word-processing document, project it onto the IWB screen, and continue with the lesson plans as if they were projected on a noninteractive screen. The important point here is that one can project and interact with anything on the IWB that is on the computer screen.

> **Teacher Tip!**
>
> Teachers can check the spelling in an entire IWB presentation no matter how many slides it has by choosing the *Check Spelling* option from the Edit menu.

Setting the Stage

The first step to an effective lesson is to tell students what they are going to learn. This task may be accomplished in many ways, and the method may vary from lesson to lesson, class to class, and teacher to teacher. Regardless of a teacher's technique, an interactive whiteboard can contribute to this initial step of the lesson plan.

Many teachers pose an essential question to help set the stage for learning. According to Wiggins, essential questions "get at matters of deep and enduring understanding." They are "proactive and multilayered questions that reveal the richness and complexities of a subject" (1998, 28). For example, a seventh-grade teacher might pose this question related to the Common Core State Standards for Mathematics: "Do random samples adequately represent a population?" Figure 4.2 lists attributes of essential questions as they relate to teaching and learning.

Figure 4.2 Attributes of Essential Questions

> A question is essential when it:
> - Causes genuine and relevant inquiry into the big ideas and core content
> - Provokes deep thought, lively discussion, sustained inquiry, and new understanding as well as more questions
> - Requires students to consider alternatives, weigh evidence, support their ideas, and justify their answers
> - Stimulates vital, ongoing rethinking of big ideas, assumptions, and prior lessons
> - Sparks meaningful connections with prior learning and personal experiences
> - Naturally recurs, creating opportunities for transfer to other situations and subjects
>
> (Wiggins 2007)

Rather than posing an essential question, some teachers prefer to simply state the lesson objective. The Common Core State Standards, individual state standards, and/or district standards may determine these objectives. By posting an objective on the first page of an IWB lesson (e.g., *Students will use random sampling to draw inferences about a population.*), every student who enters the class will know at a glance exactly what the intended learning or practice is for the day.

Often a teacher's essential questions, objectives, or topics are listed on the board at the front of the room. Remember, many things a whiteboard can do, an interactive whiteboard can do better! Teachers who use their interactive whiteboard's software to write their lesson plans can include a pull tab listing essential questions, lesson objectives, or review questions. When displaying the lesson plan page on the interactive whiteboard, the essential questions or objectives can be pulled onto the screen at the start of the lesson and then be hidden from view during the lesson. The example in Figure 4.3 shows how one teacher used a pull tab to write the essential questions for a lesson. The second tab, titled *Vocabulary*, lists the terms students will know by the end of the lesson.

Figure 4.3 Sample IWB Page with a Pull Tab for Essential Questions

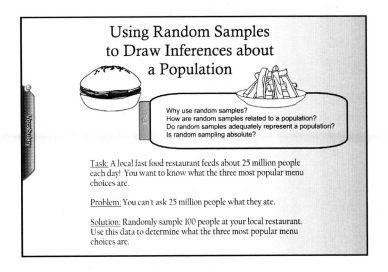

Teacher Tip!

Teachers can pose an essential or probing question at the top of an IWB page and use a screen to hide the bottom part of the page, which might have information they wish not to reveal just yet. After students have responded to the initial question, remove the screen to continue with the lesson.

However, there are times when using a regular dry-erase whiteboard or chart paper is preferable to the IWB. For example, if the teacher is creating something that should be kept for student reference, such as a diagram of important vocabulary, using chart paper adds permanence so the students can refer to the material throughout the school day. If the vocabulary chart was created on the IWB, it would visually disappear as soon as something else was displayed on the board or when the projector was turned off. It is important for teachers to choose the best tool to use for the intended purpose of the lesson.

Engaging Student Thinking

Once the teacher has focused the students on an objective or question, the next step in an effective lesson is to "hook" students. In order for learning to occur, students must be engaged in the content. This stage of an effective lesson offers just a brief hint of the learning to come. Engaging activities are quick and simple; they do not require a lot of preparation, but they do offer a lot of interest. Many students are not interested in a topic simply because they have not been engaged in the subject matter. The use of an interactive whiteboard can bring even the most abstract or what students consider to be immeasurably boring subject matter to life with a simple tap of the board.

Posing a Question

A simple way to engage students with a lesson's content is to pose a philosophical or open-ended question that may provoke an emotional response or cause students to take a position on an issue. Then, once students have a chance to think about the question, they can post their ideas to see whether their initial thoughts and opinions have evolved. For example, primary students might be asked *What makes a good friend?* The students or the teacher can write or type the students' ideas on the IWB page (see Figure 4.4). After reading a book with this theme, such as *Frog and Toad Are Friends* by Arnold Lobel (1979), the page can be revisited. Students can build on their initial ideas and write a story about an experience they shared with a friend, compare their friend to either Frog or Toad, or write an essay to explain why their friend is the best friend in the world, drawing on their ideas and those suggested in the book. A U.S. History teacher may gain students' attention by asking *Would you rather be a Tory or a Patriot, and why?* before a lesson on the Revolutionary War.

Figure 4.4 Prereading Brainstorming Activity

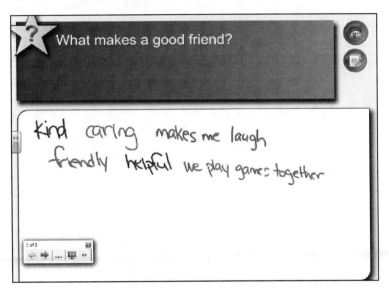

Using Realia and Primary Sources

Another way to grab students' attention at the start of a lesson is to display a piece of realia or a primary-source document, a picture, a short video, or a recent news clip related to the objectives of the lesson. An IWB is well-suited for all of these ideas. When a teacher finds an appropriate picture, video, or other media file on the Internet, he or she simply needs to bookmark it, and/or download and link it to an IWB page to find it easily when needed. Of course, an IWB cannot replicate experiences with real objects such as a Native American basket or a fossil, or create a windstorm in the classroom for students to experience. But, the Internet can share with students many otherwise unreachable objects and experiences. For example, when learning about the solar system or the universe, teachers can start every day's lesson with a visit to the NASA website, which is updated daily. Students can begin class by reading a feature article, looking at the day's top pictures, listening to a podcast, or checking in live with NASA (http://www.nasa.gov).

IWB Tips *from an expert*

During a unit on Lewis and Clark, a fifth-grade teacher downloaded a map of the United States from the Internet and placed it into an IWB document. After researching the routes of Lewis and Clark, student pairs took turns coming to the IWB to draw the westward and return routes in different colors. By duplicating the IWB page containing the map before each student pair started, the teacher was able to save all the student work for later review. Students could also come back after additional lessons on Lewis and Clark and add other elements to the maps. This was a very engaging activity for the students, allowing for a large kinesthetic venue to practice and show what they had learned. As the unit moved along, students were proactive in asking the teacher to return to their maps to add new ideas.

Preassessment

Gauging students' prior knowledge and identifying their misconceptions is an important preassessment activity. One way to accomplish this is with an activity such as a K-W-L chart. Teachers can use a modified "text category sort" template from the IWB software or project a PDF or word-processing file of a K-W-L chart. Students and teachers can use the pen or typing tools to record and save students' ideas in the *K* column. Another way to gauge students' misconceptions is to engage them with a simple word or picture sort, using a template also available with the IWB software. Figure 4.5 shows a prelearning activity in which middle-school students sorted biotic and abiotic factors. This activity took only a few minutes of class time at the start of a lesson. Students were able to check their ideas instantly, leading them to wonder about the mistakes they had made and provoking them to investigate why they made those errors.

Figure 4.5 Sorting Activity

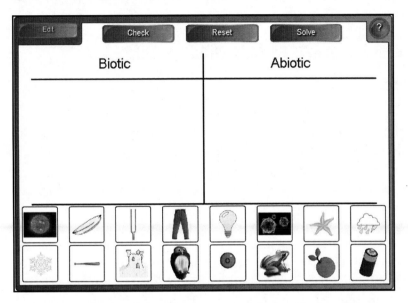

Developing Concepts and Skills

Today's educators are challenged to teach for depth and breadth. *Depth* refers to a student's understanding of a topic beyond memorizing facts, vocabulary terms, or algorithms. Instead, students explore ideas to make personal connections to information, make qualifiable and quantifiable observations, or discover or uncover some process or procedure. In essence, they derive their own meaning to bring understanding to a topic or skill. *Breadth* refers to the vast and sometimes insurmountable quantity of information that teachers are expected to cover in their courses. Unfortunately, when teachers attempt to address too much material during instruction, they speed through topics and tend to lose the depth of understanding. Likewise, if they try to teach only for depth, their narrow focus might cause them to ignore or inadvertently overlook related information that students might find particularly interesting.

With the need to teach both deeply and broadly, teachers must first determine the essential "big ideas," or essential questions surrounding a particular unit of study. Once this has been communicated to students and their interest has been piqued, the teacher can lead students down a learning path that has instructional value and also allows students to explore and learn concepts and information through what Madeline Hunter referred to as "input" (1982). Interactive whiteboards are a useful tool when teaching for depth and breadth.

Sharing Text

One way to develop concepts and skills is through reading stories or informational passages. For example, students might read a story or graphic novel that has been downloaded or is streamed electronically. Many companies offer free or affordable "electronic books," or eBooks (see Appendix C). An eBook is one that can be viewed and read on a computer or a special eBook reader. Since eBooks can be viewed on a computer, they can be projected onto an interactive whiteboard. Yet another reading option open to students is to read an interactive story or text. Students can have stories read to them, watch animated illustrations in the storybook pages, type in character names, or interact with objects in the storybook pages when they read interactive stories. Finally, students can access what the social studies field refers to as primary- and secondary-source documents. Primary sources are original documents, creative works, or relics or artifacts that give the reader or observer an insight into history. They include, but are not limited to, the Declaration of Independence, letters handwritten by westward travelers from 1840, historical maps, and copies of famous speeches. Secondary sources are any accounts of history written by others who were not there. These include, but are not limited to, encyclopedia entries, biographies, critiques, magazine articles about past events, or commentaries. And of course, any informational texts that are available online can be displayed using an interactive whiteboard.

Teachers today have what seems to be an unlimited pool of fiction and informational text resources from which to choose for instruction. The benefit of using an interactive whiteboard for reading is the fact that students can apply effective comprehension strategies such as highlighting and responding to text without danger of destroying the text resource. While reading, students have access to all the tools that accompany the IWB, such as highlighters, pens, and sticky notes. When reading fiction, students can highlight any story or text features following the teacher's direction, such as the main characters, the setting, or words that follow a certain rule such as doubling the consonant before adding *-ed* or *-ing*. Likewise, students can use the Pen tool to circle or underline strong verbs or words the author uses to express *said* (e.g., *announced, screeched, sighed*, etc.). When reading nonfiction text, students can use the sticky-note option to record thoughts or responses to the information or toggle back and forth between the text and an electronic graphic organizer to record and subsequently print notes about the information. Teachers can demonstrate how to take notes by using the IWB to complete a digital graphic organizer of the presented information by using a software program such as Kidspiration® or Inspiration®. The whole class will be engaged in organizing the content, and they can benefit from collaborating on their thinking.

IWB Tips

from an expert

During a recent social studies unit that included the study of Abraham Lincoln and George Washington, a first-grade teacher had her students brainstorm words that described these two leaders. Each student listed five to 20 words. Students listed many of the same words, but several were only written once. The teacher had each student come up to the IWB and tally their words so that when they were finished, there was a clean visual record of all the words and how many times each word occurred for each leader. The teacher then took the words (and their frequencies) and used the word cloud website Wordle (http://www.wordle.net) to create a unique word cloud for both Lincoln and Washington. The word clouds were then inserted back into the IWB file adjacent to the word tallies. This provided a meaningful visual opportunity for the students to see how the frequency of their words led to the different sizes of the words in the Wordle. This activity could have been done without an IWB, but using it as a student-centered tool allowed for engaged students, resource organization, and a powerful visual display.

> **Great Idea!**
>
> An IWB will save or print anything in writing. IWB notes can be:
>
> - Saved in a file on a shared server that students can access
> - Linked to a teacher's or school's website or blog
> - Printed and distributed to students prior to a lesson so that students can engage more fully with the lesson and add their own ideas

Interactive Games, Manipulatives, and Simulations

Another way to develop concepts and skills with the use of an interactive whiteboard is to have students participate in interactive online games, activities, and simulations. Many mathematics teachers like to use manipulatives to help students develop conceptual understanding of mathematics topics, such as skip-counting, division, comparing fractions, and sorting by multiple attributes. One instructional strategy presented by Fisher and Frey (2008) is the "I do, we do, you do" approach. This strategy is particularly useful when teaching students new skills and concepts in mathematics. Teachers can find a variety of math manipulatives for meeting a number of instructional objectives from one of many websites that offer virtual manipulatives (see Appendix C). Once projected, the teacher may use the virtual manipulatives to demonstrate the concept for students and then allow students to use the projected manipulatives to demonstrate their understanding in front of the class. If tangible manipulatives are not available, students who are not quite ready to work on their own ("you do") can come to the IWB for additional practice with the teacher before working independently to practice the skill.

IWB Tips *from an expert*

During a math lesson on place value, a second-grade teacher engaged students using virtual base-ten blocks on the IWB. She inserted digital images of the place-value blocks (hundreds flats, tens bars, and ones cubes) into an IWB file and used the "Infinite Cloner" function on her SMART™ Board ("Drag a Copy" on Promethean boards) so students could have access to as many of the base-ten blocks as they needed. The teacher used this IWB file to both model the process for students (while they did it at their desks with physical manipulatives) and then during guided practice as pairs of students worked problems at the board. This allowed students a break from seatwork as they took turns coming to the IWB.

One powerful instructional strategy is the use of games or simulations. Part of the learning process involves exploring, questioning, and testing ideas. Educators who embrace the constructivist approach often use games and simulations to give students opportunities to reach their own conclusions and formulate their own conceptions. Just as there are seemingly endless literature and nonfiction text resources available to students, the Internet likewise holds a slew of engaging, appropriate, and meaningful activities and simulations to help students generate their own learning. The following examples listed by subject area are just a sampling of the teaching resources available to teachers. The games and activities are versatile in that they provide activities teachers can use to first teach students ("I do") and then work alongside students ("we do") before having students practice the skill independently ("you do").

Sample Reading Activity

Use interactive materials to model how to find the main idea and details in a particular text selection. The interactive activities available at Internet4Classrooms (http://www.internet4classrooms.com) are grade-level specific. Demonstrate and guide students through any one of the reading skills listed before having students practice this skill on their own.

Sample Mathematics Activity

To help students learn how to identify fractions, use a website with an instructional tutorial and examples. The Visual Fractions website (http://www.visualfractions.com) allows teachers to choose a fraction skill (identify, rename, compare, add, subtract, multiply, or divide), decide whether to use lines or circles, and then engage in the interactive activity. Think aloud as students work through the lesson, explaining to students why they are manipulating the fractional pieces as they are, grouping objects as they are, and typing each numerator and denominator for each fractional part. Use the self-checking option to provide an explanation should the students mistakenly enter and submit the wrong answer.

Sample Science Activity

To teach students about earth-changing processes, use the online game "Shape It Up" (http://www.kineticcity.com/mindgames/warper). Students match the erosion process by looking at before-and-after illustrations of land features. Then, have them determine the length of time each earth-altering process takes. By playing the game, students identify several forces of nature and determine their effects and the time they take to change the earth. By engaging in the activity and taking notes about each process (see Figure 4.6), students learn about the forces that change the earth.

Figure 4.6 "Shape It Up" Notes

Force	Effect	Length of Time
water	river through desert	100 years
volcano	new volcano on ocean floor	100 years
glacier	valley	10,000 years
wind	eroded bluff	20,000,000 years

Sample Social Studies Activity

Use the online interactive activity "Opportunity Cost Shop" from Econopolis (http://library.thinkquest.org/3901) to help students understand opportunity cost in economics. Read about and discuss this idea with students and then calculate an opportunity cost using the online example. To help students secure their thinking with regard to this concept, have them summarize the activity in their social studies notebooks and explain how their personal-opportunity cost calculations compare with yours.

Videos

Another highly valuable instructional strategy to help students develop concepts and skills is to show a streamed or downloaded video related to a particular topic. Videos, when used appropriately and meaningfully, broaden students' understanding of otherwise abstract concepts, especially in science and social studies. The benefit of using an interactive whiteboard to display videos is that the teacher can pause the film at any point to discuss a particular point and use the IWB software program and tools to emphasize important points, take notes, jot questions, or summarize information. After the video is viewed, these points, notes, questions, and summaries may be printed and distributed for students to use as study guides.

Stop and Think

- What types of teaching activities do you use now to develop concepts and skills?
- How do these activities compare with those discussed in this section?
- In what way(s) can the use of an IWB enhance how you develop concepts and skills with your students (in any subject area)?

Practice and Review

Once students have learned a new skill, they must have opportunities to practice and apply it. Students also need opportunities to review what they have learned. Appendix C lists some interactive websites that offer students opportunities to practice skills in an engaging fashion for reading and mathematics. Teachers can also conduct an online search of the specific skill they want students to practice on the IWB. It usually does not take long to find numerous options for practice of almost any skill through the Internet. Teachers should always preview these lessons prior to demonstrating them for students.

For review purposes, the IWB software program likely has ready-made learning templates that teachers can use to create review sessions related to any topic. For example, the activity in Figure 4.7 shows a teacher's use of a notes template to write statements for her first-grade class's review of one place in their community, the park. When the page first opens, each numbered space is blank. The statements show when the button number is tapped. By clicking the Edit button, the teacher can add any additional details that the students remember about each main idea. This is the ideal review activity before students continue their study of other places in the community.

Figure 4.7 Review Notes about Places in the Community: The Park

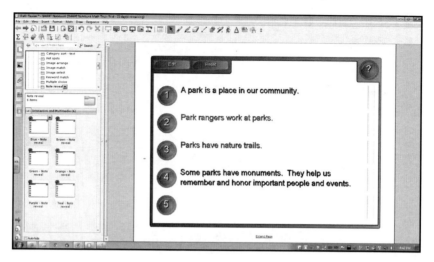

Just as online interactive games can be engaging instructional strategies, they can also provide review and practice opportunities for students across the content areas. For example, students can practice homophone pairs in pictures and in context by playing the "Vocabulary Homophone" game from *Learning Today* (http://www.learningtoday.com/player/swf/Vocabulary_Homophones_L2_V1_T4a.swf). Of course, the Internet is not the only tool in the box. Teachers can always access a favorite computer program available on their network or on a CD to review and practice skills. By projecting the program onto the IWB, the whole class can join in the fun.

IWB Tips *from an expert*

A fifth-grade teacher uses the IWB to introduce the Internet-based math games that are part of his district-adopted mathematics curriculum. Many of these games pedagogically lend themselves quite well to the interactive environment of the IWB (exceptions to this are games that require heavy keyboard use). While he is introducing a game to the class on the IWB, student volunteers are called upon to do the clicking and dragging. While most students use classroom computers to access the games, the IWB is often made available for pairs of students to play the same games.

Assessing Student Learning

The education world has divided the domain of student assessment into two categories: formative assessment and summative assessment. Formative assessment happens all day, every day, in every classroom. They are assessments teachers continuously make to gauge their students' progress toward skill or concept mastery (see Chapter 1). Indeed, if a teacher waits until the end of a unit or lesson to "test" students' understanding of the objectives, it is too late to modify instruction to help students achieve goals. The critical moments of identifying trouble areas and providing additional support and instruction when and where it is needed will have already passed. A teacher who uses observation, interviewing, or ungraded activities or quizzes to help him or her know who "got it" and who did not is using formative assessment strategies. In doing so, this teacher can provide instructional support through reteaching and additional practice to continue to develop and extend learning.

> "The true value of assessment is its ability to help educators make accurate and timely inferences about student progress so that they can modify instruction accordingly."
>
> —Ainsworth 2007, 80

Summative assessments are more formal in nature. This is usually the process through which teachers derive grades. With summative assessments, teachers check students' mastery level at the completion of a unit of study. Summative assessments typically take the form of some sort of test. Projects can also act as summative assessments. To accurately assess students' understanding of a particular topic, a rubric or grading scale that clearly identifies the criteria upon which students will be evaluated must be included.

While assessments have traditionally taken the form of paper-pencil tasks, an interactive whiteboard is an excellent tool to assist teachers in assessing students' understanding of the subject matter they have taught.

Formative Assessments

The least-formal manner in which to formatively assess students is through observation. This may be accomplished by observing students' level of class participation or watching students as they complete guided practice or independent work. As a lesson involving an interactive whiteboard unfolds, teachers can make observations about students' interest level, participation level, and comfort level as they work to meet lesson objectives. Then, as students are engaged in independent or collaborative practice, teachers can reflect on their mental notes and provide support to students who may need more focused attention.

Another option for quick formative assessment is the use of "exit cards" (or a "ticket out the door") to help teachers gauge students' levels of success in meeting a lesson's objectives. One way to implement this strategy with an IWB is to revisit the essential questions or lesson objectives, which might have been stored away using a pull tab. Then, students write on a note card or slip of paper to respond in writing to any one or more of the questions or objectives. This should take at most three minutes at the end of the class period. Teachers then collect the cards to review and analyze the students' responses to determine who "has it," who is "getting it," and who is completely lost. Teachers can return the cards at the start of the next day's class period to act as a review of yesterday's learning. They simply repost the essential questions or lesson objectives on the IWB, and let students talk with each other for one or two minutes about what they learned the previous day, using their cards as memory joggers.

Some teachers like to have their students write regularly in learning logs, notebooks, or journals. An interactive whiteboard can help with this, too. Teachers can simply create a page with a list of general questions (see Figure 4.8) or specific questions that are relevant to the topic of study. Questions should be open-ended and allow students to make personal connections. Attach this question list page to an IWB lesson or minimize it on the desktop to pull up when needed. Let students respond to one or more questions in their journals as time allows, generally for five to ten minutes. Periodically collect the journals to review. Or collect and read a few each day from different students. Journals offer insight into students' thinking and provide a better understanding of their progress toward mastering the lesson's objectives and learning the content.

Figure 4.8 Sample Journal Questions

- What did you learn that you did not know before?
- How might you use the information you learned another time?
- Why is this information important to know?
- What is the most important thing to remember about this topic?
- How can you relate this information to someone or something else?
- What does this information make you think about?
- How does this information make you feel?
- What questions do you still have about this topic?
- If this topic were an animal, what kind of animal would it be, and why?
- If this topic could talk to you right now, what would it say? How would you respond?

Teacher Tip!

Teachers often run out of time to conclude a lesson with a journal prompt. Use a timer to sound an alarm five to ten minutes before the end of the class period. At that point, display the review questions (even if the lesson is not quite complete) to allow students to reflect on the information provided thus far.

Much formative assessment occurs during guided and independent practice. This is because students are trying out a newly learned skill for the first time. At this time, the teacher can identify students who need more challenging work, those who need additional practice with the same skill, and those who have gaps in background knowledge that must be addressed. IWB practice activities provide time for students to practice new skills in a safe environment with instant feedback. While students are practicing, the teacher can make notes to himself or herself regarding students who need additional guided practice before working independently. To increase the level of engagement among students, teachers can have each student record his or her answers to IWB practice problems on an individual whiteboard, using a dry-erase marker. Once the individual boards are presented to the teacher, he or she can get an instant snapshot of the class's progress toward the lesson's objectives. Then, the teacher can reveal the correct response for students to self-check their work. Once a majority of the class is successful with the guided-practice problems, the teacher can assign independent work and assist students who continued to respond incorrectly to the guided-practice problems on the IWB. (For information about self-checking activities, see Chapter 3. For information about conducting small-group lessons at the interactive whiteboard, see Chapter 7.)

Student Response Systems

Student response systems are a piece of IWB technology that is ideal for implementing formative assessment. Teachers who have a student response system available can design and create mini-assessments or quizzes to give to students periodically throughout a unit. The teacher can analyze these results in order to determine students' level of content mastery before the students "officially" demonstrate their knowledge in a summative assessment. The advantage of using teacher-made mini-assessments is that the teacher can assess each specific skill with its own quiz. Many published tests and quizzes include questions related to several skills or topics, requiring the teacher to conduct an item analysis of the tests to determine the skill(s) with which the class excelled and the skill(s) with which the class struggled. For example, a teacher might want to know how well his or her students understand contractions. This concept might be one of three embedded within a reading selection, and the textbook publisher might not provide an assessment to check students' understanding of this one particular skill. Instead, more formal (summative) assessments might include 20 questions related to contractions, pronouns, and superlatives. Two students might both score 16 out of 20 on a publisher's test but may have completely different levels of mastery on contractions. Where the first student may have only missed one or two questions per skill, the second student may have missed four out of five questions on contractions. The first student exhibits a modicum of mastery for all three skills, whereas the second student's score would indicate that he or she mastered pronouns and superlatives but not contractions. Using a student response system, the teacher could create three separate mini-assessments (one for each skill) to administer to students *before* the final summative assessment and be able to provide additional instructional support when it is needed.

The use of student response systems with an IWB not only gives feedback to the teacher about his or her students' skill acquisition but can also provide immediate feedback to students about their own learning. Immediately after responses are entered, the program can show the percentage of students responding to each answer choice as well as identify the correct answer. The practice of providing meaningful feedback to students in a timely manner is well documented as a best practice by researchers (Bangert-Drowns et al. 1991; Hattie and Timperley 2007; Kluger and DeNisi 1996). Additionally, this simple process is highly motivating for students. Even reluctant learners strive to "beat the system." Students are driven to answer correctly for their own personal satisfaction (they want to see that they answered correctly) as well as to help raise the overall class's percent-correct score.

IWB Tips *from an expert*

The student response systems also provide teachers the opportunity to ask questions "on the fly." Immediately after students respond, the teacher has data that can inform his or her instruction. I was recently in a third-grade classroom helping with a lesson on adding fractions. At one point, the teacher turned to me and said (so that students could also hear) that she thought perhaps some students were confusing the two terms *numerator* and *denominator*. Then, she used the student response system to poll the students on which number in a fraction is the numerator and which one is the denominator. As it turned out, she was right—thirty-five percent of the students answered incorrectly (they had forgotten or confused the two terms). The teacher immediately spent about three minutes reviewing the vocabulary and concepts before the students returned to work. During this process, the IWB was used to display the formative assessment question, the class results, and the subsequent reteaching.

Student response systems are also useful for students to provide confidential feedback to their teachers with regard to how they perceive their own learning. This process allows students to evaluate and share how they feel their learning is progressing. Wiggins (1998) identifies this process of self-assessment as a critical and essential component to ongoing feedback for both students and teachers. What does this look like? In the aforementioned language arts example, assessment questions might read:

1. I know all about contractions.   A. yes   B. no   C. kind of

2. I know all about pronouns.   A. yes   B. no   C. kind of

3. I know how to compare things.   A. yes   B. no   C. kind of

After the assessment, the teacher can review each student's response and conference with students, if needed, regarding their perspectives on their progress. As with any formative assessment, the teacher can then strategically provide instructional support (or learning extensions).

Summative Assessments

Student Response Systems

In addition to formative assessments, student response systems offer summative assessment opportunities as well. If teachers plan to give students a formal end-of-unit multiple-choice test, this technology can be extremely useful. The test can be projected on the IWB, and students can use the response system to "click in" and submit their answer to a multiple-choice question. The program scores students' responses as correct or incorrect and may even upload the scores into a grading program, thus eliminating the need for the teacher to hand-score tests.

Some researchers caution against the use of multiple-choice tests as a means to assess student learning (Popham 2008; Stiggins et al. 2006). When analyzed, how does a summative multiple-choice test help the teacher evaluate student learning? Did students really know the subject matter, or were they good guessers? One way around this testing dilemma is to have students write explanations of why they did or did not choose a particular answer. (In this situation, an IWB is useful for the teacher to project the test and have students respond electronically, but students will need paper and pencil to write their justifications.) This strategy holds students more accountable for their responses. Assessing students digitally through a student response system saves paper and time, two valuable commodities in today's educational system.

Projects

If teachers assign summative assessment projects, students who complete digital projects can utilize the interactive features of the program's software when they share their project with the class, and the class can interact with their presentation. Since an interactive whiteboard works with any multimedia program, students can embellish their presentations with animations, slide transitions, audio or media files, or embedded website links. For example, students can use an online poster-making program, such as *Glogster* (http://www.edu.glogster.com), to design and create brilliant electronic posters following the criteria the teacher sets for them. Then, they can use the IWB to actively present their work.

> **Teacher Tip!**
>
> When assigning any project, be sure to prepare and share the criteria upon which students will be evaluated *before* they begin working. Project-specific rubrics and checklists are all appropriate and useful evaluation tools.

Cross-Curricular Extensions

Often teachers want to extend concepts students have studied by linking them to other content areas. There are various and sundry ways to expand learning across the curriculum. Students may work in collaborative groups to research and report on a topic in a related content area and prepare a visual representation (a three-dimensional model or poster) to demonstrate their learning. Some teachers might engage their class in reader's theater to explore an idea through drama. Or they might link a concept to literature or current events to expand on students' thinking. Regardless of the approach, the use of an IWB can aid in cross-curricular extensions. These inquiry experiences allow students to apply learning in novel and unique situations. They engage students and help them maintain a high level of energy, both high-yield attributes in today's classrooms (Marzano 2003).

- Have students enact a play or reenact a historical event. Use the IWB to display backgrounds for each scene in reader's theater. As scenes change in the script, the teacher simply presses the forward button on the IWB software to move to the next scene.

- Have students conduct an "on the scene interview" as news reporters who have traveled to a different time or place to meet a historical figure. A photo of a historical scene can be displayed on the IWB.

- Take students on a virtual field trip.

- Videoconference with an expert.

- Have students post a summary of their learning to a classroom blog. Then, share the blog entries with the class using the IWB the next day. Add to the blog as a class following a discussion of one or two postings.

> "Role-playing and simulations require students to improvise, using the information available to them. In the process, they encourage critical thinking and cooperative learning. These teaching tools can also be effective in helping students clarify attitudes and ideologies and make connections between abstract concepts and real-world events."
>
> —Enhancing Education 2011, under "Role-Playing and Simulations"

Chapter Summary

This chapter explores the parts of an effective lesson plan and how an interactive whiteboard can play a vital role in each stage of a teacher's lesson-plan development. The ultimate goal of any lesson is to have students learn new skills and understand new content. How teachers accomplish this is unique. Every teacher has his or her own teaching style, and each class has its own culture and climate. Some instructional strategies that work with one group of students or in one grade level may not necessarily work with another group of students or another grade level. However, the use of an interactive whiteboard as an integral part of the daily lesson plan development should help keep the pace of the lesson moving along, and it should help teachers keep their students' interest in the topic at hand. Its versatility and usefulness make the IWB a valuable instructional tool teachers can use any time of day for multifarious purposes and support of the highly effective instructional strategies they already use.

Reflection Questions

1. What do you consider to be the most important part or stage of a lesson? How do you plan to use your IWB in the development of this part of the lesson?

2. In what ways will the use of an interactive whiteboard help you design and deliver effective lessons? How is this different from more traditional approaches to teaching and learning?

3. How do you believe your students' response to lessons will change with the use of an interactive whiteboard as part of their instructional routine?

Chapter 5

Getting Started with the Interactive Whiteboard

> *"It may be hard for an egg to turn into a bird: it would be a jolly sight harder for it to learn to fly while remaining an egg. We are like eggs at present. And you cannot go on indefinitely being just an ordinary, decent egg. We must be hatched or go bad."*
>
> —C.S. Lewis 2001, 170

Teachers must have the courage, determination, and drive to hatch their IWB from its box and let their lessons soar! Taking the first step may be challenging, but the reward is worth it. This chapter presents simple techniques and strategies that even less-than-tech-savvy teachers can try on an IWB with confidence in any one or more subjects. If teachers remember to start small, trying one new IWB feature at a time, their confidence and competence will grow. Eventually, users will have an entire server folder bursting with lesson ideas. Simple IWB lessons can gradually evolve into more complex activities with the addition of an advanced function (see Chapter 6).

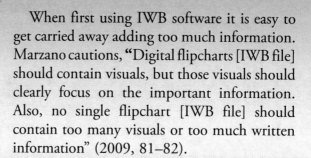

When first using IWB software it is easy to get carried away adding too much information. Marzano cautions, "Digital flipcharts [IWB file] should contain visuals, but those visuals should clearly focus on the important information. Also, no single flipchart [IWB file] should contain too many visuals or too much written information" (2009, 81–82).

Beginning Routine

The following ideas for kicking off the day or class period with the IWB will motivate students to arrive promptly and ready to learn.

Morning Calendar

Primary teachers can stream an online calendar program from a website such as http://www.Starfall.com or they can use IWB software to create their own daily calendar routine. Students can recite the date, review the days of the week, identify the day before and the day after today, and count days.

Morning Message

Greet students with a welcoming message, or post a warm-up assignment for students to complete when they first arrive to class. In the primary grades, this might be a simple task or the daily routine, such as unpacking backpacks, sharpening pencils, and completing morning work. In the intermediate grades, this might take the form of a journal prompt or question related to the previous day's instruction.

> **Teacher Tip!**
>
> If the IWB software comes with a "scrolling banner" template, teachers can type routine, repetitive messages in the banner, and then list daily, specific directions for students on the IWB page.

Check In

Students can help with the chore of taking attendance with the IWB. Devise a way for students to check in when they enter the room. They might simply drag their name into a shape. They might delete or erase their name from the board. They might drag their name into a graphic organizer, such as a Venn diagram. For example, students could drag their name into one of the Venn spaces to show whether they have brothers, sisters, both, or neither, or whether they like fruits, vegetables, both, or neither.

IWB Tips from an expert

The IWB can be used to assist in taking attendance as the students enter the room. This is an extremely simple task in terms of setup time for the teacher, and it engages the students with a question at the same time. For example, when the students enter the room, they might see a question such as *Do you agree with the new lunchtime rules in the cafeteria?* Each of the students' names is also on the IWB file as draggable items (each name is in its own text field). There is also a simple graphic organizer with two columns, one labeled *yes* and the other *no*. As students are putting away their things, turning in homework, and dropping off notes with the teacher, they also stop by the IWB and drag their name into the appropriate column. When students are finished, the teacher has a visual of the students who are absent in addition to some discussion material to start the day. The content is easily changed from day to day, as the teacher only has to change the question and perhaps the labels for the columns.

Agendas

Posting a daily schedule satisfies students' curiosity about the events planned for a day or a class period. Teachers can create an IWB slide or page just for this purpose, and minimize it when it is not needed. Or, they can create a pull tab listing the day's events and hide the tab once they begin instruction. (See Chapter 4 for information about creating pull tabs.) Either way, teachers have ready access to the classwork and assignments students are to complete throughout the day.

Classroom Management

Attending to tasks on an interactive whiteboard is motivating to most students in and of itself. However, engaging with an IWB can also be used as a reward when it becomes part of a classroom behavior plan. Teachers can use opportunities to work at the IWB as a reward for model classroom behavior. These positive reinforcement strategies help both novice and experienced teachers maintain a positive and respectful classroom atmosphere.

> **Teacher Quote**
>
> *"I downloaded, for a small price, an online interactive Monopoly™ game. I modified it so that the game pieces were the students' names and the spaces were small rewards, such as a free homework pass, a trip to the treasure box, a small treat, or student choice. Each day, when students turn in their homework, they get to roll a die and move their game piece. If they don't bring their homework, or if it is incomplete, they do not get to move their name. We only need about five minutes for this at the beginning of each day. It's a win-win. I collect their homework, and they get to move their game piece for a small reward. My students look forward to doing their homework!"*
>
> —Rebecca Standridge,
> Third-Grade Teacher

Language Arts

There are myriad ways in which teachers can use their interactive whiteboards during language arts instruction. The ideas that follow represent some of the many opportunities for integrating the IWB into language arts instruction.

> **Self-Checking Options:** An IWB page can use one of many self-checking options.
>
> - Use an interactive template that allows for self-checking.
>
> - Mark over the correct answer with a marker color that matches the background color. Then, students can erase the marker to check their answers. (See Figure 5.1.)
>
> - Cover a word or answer with a filled rectangle. Students move the rectangle out of the way or delete it to reveal the correct word or answer.
>
> - Use the screen cover to hide the correct answer below each question. Pull the screen down after students respond to the question to see the correct answer.

Figure 5.1 Vocabulary Practice Using the Eraser to Self-Check

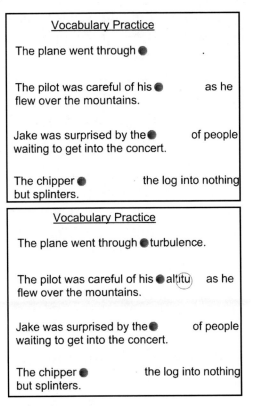

The eraser tool is used to reveal the correct answers.

Grammar, Spelling, and Punctuation

- Create or stream a self-checking beginning or ending letter-picture matching game.
- Create an alphabetical-order game using a sequencing template, or stream one from the Internet that matches the students' skill level.
- Create a write-in, self-checking, or matching contraction activity.
- Create a matching compound word game.
- Create a noun/proper noun word-sort activity or a parts-of-speech sorting activity. Write original, creative sentences with words from the sorting activity on a second IWB page.

- Display different types of sentences (statements, questions, and exclamatory sentences) with the ending punctuation hidden. Have students use a Self-Checker tool to choose the correct end mark for each sentence.

- Display sentences that require editing (sentences with intentional spelling, grammar, or punctuation errors). Use the Highlighter and Pen tools to edit the sentences as a class.

- Display sentences and clauses. Have students use a self-checking tool to correctly identify each.

- Create a matching game for rhyming words. Add multiple pages, each with its own base word to rhyme, to allow students to practice several different rhyming patterns during one practice session.

- Stream a word-building program for students to practice onset and rime, ending sounds, medial sounds, digraphs, and diphthongs.

- Create a self-check grammar-related activity, such as one to identify proper nouns, plurals, verb tenses, helping verbs, or word endings (see Figure 5.2).

Figure 5.2 Self-Checking Activity: "Change –y to –ie Before Adding –s"

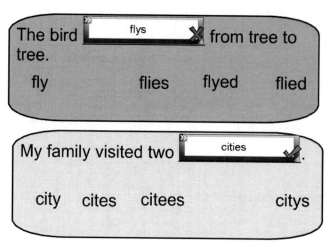

- Use a word list template (or create one on a blank IWB page) to brainstorm a list of nouns, verbs, adjectives, or adverbs. These lists can be saved and referenced during writing instruction. Challenge students to find or think of unusual words that will energize their writing.

- Allow students to use the IWB at a literacy center to practice their spelling words. Up to four students can write on the board at one time (one student for each pen) while another student (the "teacher") calls out the words and checks the answers. One student assigned as the "eraser" erases the board to be ready for the next word. After two or three words, the students switch pen colors or switch roles so that each student has a turn as the "eraser" and the "teacher."

IWB Tips *from an expert*

During literacy centers, the second-grade teachers have students working on several different independent activities while they meet with individuals for targeted instruction or goal-setting conferences. In one of these independent activities, students write words on the IWB. Each student has a list of words they are working on at any given time, and they pull from this list during the IWB activity. Working in pairs at the board, students simply take turns writing their words two or three times each, in a different color each time, and drawing a picture to represent the word. Students are encouraged to use the words orally in a sentence. When they have both finished writing their lists, they switch to a different activity and a new student pair comes to the board.

Writing

- Create a handwriting practice page using IWB software dashed letters (see the resource library). Students may trace the letters "in the air" from their seats by pointing at the board and following along as the teacher uses the Pen tool to trace the letters on the board. After adequate "air" practice, students may practice writing the letters on paper or individual whiteboards at their seats.

- Display a "boring" sentence on a blank page or slide. Have students add descriptive words and/or phrases. Retype the sentence on a new page or slide to print, or handwrite it on a sentence strip to post in the classroom.

- Display a paragraph that requires revisions, such as more dynamic verbs, specific nouns, "showing" sentences, or additional details. Use the Highlighter and Pen tools to revise the paragraph as a class.

- Display a story or essay starter using a notebook-paper background. Have students work collaboratively or independently to continue the story or essay, using paper and pencil. Model for the class how the essay or story might continue on the IWB, using the Pen tools. Then, have students type their ideas during their literacy center time. Open students' files and display them for the class when students share their writing.

- Use students' work to discuss effective writing strategies. Project one story or essay to discuss as a class. (For information on how to project paper documents, see Chapter 6.) Use the Highlighter or Pen tools to identify strong verbs, "showing" sentences, or other effective writing strategies that the teacher wishes to point out to students.

- Keep pages, slides, or documents as a digital database for colorful words (such as pages of words to use other than "said," "good," or "nice") or for fantastic phrases (such as figurative language or ideas discovered and recorded through literature).

- Write a class story across several slides or pages. Write the beginning on the first slide. Write the events across several additional slides. Write the conclusion on the final slide. Add interactive features, animations, or audio or media files to embellish the story. Be sure to revise and edit the original story using the Pen tools. (For information related to advanced audio features, see Chapter 6.)

- Use the IWB as an integral part of a poetry unit by reading different types of poems, creating class poems, and developing "poetic" vocabulary. Have students create their own poem using a word processing or slide show program, or other electronic software of choice. Encourage them to use interactive features, or embellished text features. Have students use the IWB to project and share their poem with the class. (For information on how to use other software files with an IWB, see Chapter 6.)

> **Go Digital!**
>
> For fun and engaging online interactive writing activities, visit ReadWriteThink at http://readwritethink.org.

Reading

- Project a vocabulary graphic organizer, such as a word web or a Frayer model. Complete the organizer as a class on the board. Have students complete their own organizers in a notebook or on notecards to use as study guides. (For information on how to project and modify a paper document or electronic file in another software program, see Chapter 6.)

- Create a cloze activity for vocabulary terms that are part of a current reading selection.

- Create open-ended, write-in analogies for vocabulary terms. (For example, Police is to authority as sugar is to _____.)

- Introduce a text by discussing and brainstorming ideas related to the theme.

- Project a page of pictures that relate to the text in some way. Have students predict what the story will be about. Revisit this page after reading the text. Have students organize the objects in the order in which they appeared in the text.

- Use the IWB to record and save students' ideas related to the characters, setting, plot, and conclusion of a book.

- Create a story map using slides or pages for each part of the story.

- Complete a graphic organizer matched to the organization of a nonfiction text selection (e.g., main ideas and details, cause and effect, sequencing, or drawing conclusions). (For information on how to project and modify a paper document or electronic file in another software program, see Chapter 6.)

Stop and Think: Language Arts

Choose from these options to begin building a bank of IWB activities for language arts:
- Create a self-checking IWB activity for an upcoming language arts topic or for review of a skill already taught.
- Search online for a ready-made IWB reading or writing lesson to use with students.
- Find an electronic book to share with students on the IWB.
- **Challenge!** Create a series of pages or slides to use during an upcoming book study. Include a book title introductory activity, self-checking vocabulary slides, comprehension questions for students to answer, and a project related to one or more story elements or the theme of the story.

Mathematics

Research shows that students have increased achievement, especially in mathematics, when their teachers use interactive whiteboards (BECTA 2003; Miller, Glover, and Averis 2004). Developing conceptual understanding in mathematics is a highly visual endeavor, and thus instruction in this content area is especially well-suited to the use of the interactive whiteboard. One of the greatest benefits of the use of IWBs is the high level of interaction for review and practice and instant feedback so that students can correct their errors rather than practice a skill incorrectly. Appendix C lists several online, interactive math game sites where students can practice math facts, concepts, and skills in a nonthreatening yet motivating and meaningful manner. The following ideas for implementing the IWB in mathematics instruction are organized around the domains of the Grades K–5 Common Core State Standards for Mathematics.

Number and Operations

- Use Table, Drawing, and Clip Art tools to manipulate objects to demonstrate any number of numeration skills. Figure 5.3 shows red and yellow dots on a two-by-five table (ten-frame). Students manipulate the dots to show many ways to make 10.

Figure 5.3 Ten-Frame

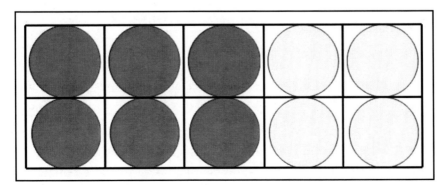

- Create a matching game for students to match a numeral to the correct number of objects, its expanded form, or its number word.

- Insert multiple objects for students to practice counting. Move the objects from one side of the board to the other as the students count them.

- Create a matching game where students correctly identify the place value of a red (or other color) numeral in a given number.

- Create a matching or self-checking computation practice page.

> **Teacher Tip!**
>
> Challenge students to increase their rate of computation by inserting an interactive stopwatch. Set the timer for a suitable length of time and then let the computer count down and alert students when time is up.

- As a class, write or insert objects on a blank page to show all the ways to represent a particular number. Intermediate students may be challenged to represent a number using multiple operations in each expression.

- Manipulate inserted images to demonstrate the concepts of addition (move objects together), subtraction (delete objects from the page), multiplication (show multiple groups or create arrays), division (move a set of objects into groups), and fractional parts of a whole (use Drawing tools to circle objects that are part of a set).

- Create a page of computation problems for students to solve on paper or on individual whiteboards. Use a digital calculator to check the answers.

- Use random generators (such as dice, numbers, and dominoes) to create chance computation problems for students to solve. Most IWB software programs contain random generators that allow you to type in numbers, words, etc. and then have the tool reveal one of the numbers or words randomly each time you click.

- Use Math tools (such as Place Value Charts, Number Lines, and Number Grids), and markers or highlighters to help students count on and count back, show multiples, skip-count, or identify odd and even numbers.

- Create a sorting activity for students to distinguish between prime and composite numbers.

- Search for a ready-to-go online interactive numeration or computation lesson to project onto the IWB.

Geometry

- Create a self-checking or matching activity for students in which they identify the number of vertices, edges, or faces of shapes and objects. Figure 5.4 shows a "Balloon Pop" activity in which students identify the correct number of cubes.

Figure 5.4 "Balloon Pop" Geometry Self-checking Activity

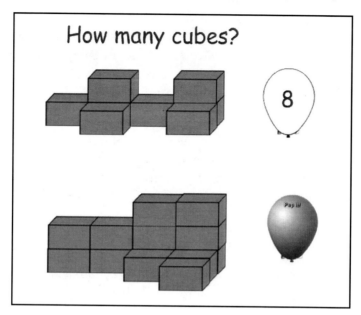

- Use Drawing and Math tools to illustrate vocabulary terms such as *parallel, perpendicular, line, segment, right angle, obtuse, acute,* and *polygon.* Save the database of math terms to reference as needed during subsequent lessons.

- Use an Interactive Protractor tool to demonstrate and practice measuring angles.

- Use the Resizing tool to enlarge and reduce an image, and the Clone or Duplicate function to demonstrate and label the concepts of *similar* and *congruent.*

- Use a graph-paper background to investigate how the area of a rectangle changes when its perimeter changes.

- Insert an image and use the Flip function to demonstrate reflections (flips) and translations (slides). Use the Turning tool to show a rotation (turn).

- Create an activity page on which students must find the volume of several solid figures and then order them from the least volume to the greatest volume.

Measurement and Data

- Use an interactive ruler to demonstrate how to measure the length of objects.

- Create a matching or self-checking page for students to choose the right unit of measure for a particular object (e.g., varying lengths, weight, area, volume, or temperature).

- Project a page filled with random objects. Have students sort the objects according to their measurement characteristics. For example, students might sort objects by size, or they may sort them by weight. Then, they should identify the two sorting characteristics, such as *heavier than a bowling ball/lighter than a bowling ball* or *longer than a paper clip/shorter than a paper clip*.

- Create a workspace for students to calculate the perimeter of different shapes created with the Shapes tool. Label each side's length with the Typing tool. Have students calculate the perimeters on individual whiteboards and check their answers using the interactive calculator.

- Use a Thermometer tool to practice reading temperatures. Insert pictures of objects that are related to a particular temperature. For example, have students identify the minimum temperature water must have for a person to swim or to ice skate and the estimated temperature of a steaming cup of hot chocolate and a glass of milk.

- Create a matching activity for analog and digital time.

- Create a page with an inserted table or T-chart to record data. Then, use the IWB software's graphing program to show students how to graph the data.

- Type a set of data using the Text tool. Have students organize the data from least to greatest and then use the Pen tool to circle the minimum and maximum values and the Highlighter tool to highlight the median. Students can also use the Interactive Calculator to calculate the mean.

- Drag a coordinate grid to a blank page. Show students how to plot coordinates.

- Place a circle on a blank page. Use an Interactive Protractor to show students how to draw angles to represent percentages in a circle graph.

- Project database software to show students how to use other programs to record, chart, and display data. Use the Typing and Pointer tools to demonstrate how to use this software. (For information on how to use other software programs with an IWB, see Chapter 6.)

- Display a double or triple Venn diagram. Demonstrate how to group data, such as the pets students own or the vegetables students like. Label each circle in the diagram with categories, and then have students type and drag their names into the appropriate space to represent themselves. Use the completed chart to identify similarities and differences.

Operations and Algebraic Thinking

- Type, review, and save the steps to the problem-solving method (e.g., understand, plan, try, look back) on a single slide or page. Display this slide or page for review when presenting students with a new problem to solve. (Learn to link this "steps" slide to a problem on any other slide in an IWB presentation. See Chapter 6 for more information about linking slides.)

- Use IWB Drawing tools and Clip Art to demonstrate how to solve a problem by making a diagram or drawing. Save this page for review during a future lesson.

- Use a blank page to demonstrate how to solve a problem using the guess, check, and revise method.

- Use the IWB table and T-Chart tools to demonstrate how to solve a problem by making a Table to look for a pattern or make an organized list.

- Project logic problems from the Internet for students to solve.

- Project a word problem onto the IWB. Have small groups of students work collaboratively to solve the problem. Have one student share how his or her group solved the problem on a blank IWB page. Have another student from another group share a different way to solve the problem on another IWB page. Save the pages to refer to during future lessons when students need to solve a similar problem.

IWB Tips *from an expert*

As part of guided practice and independent work involving patterns, a kindergarten teacher used her IWB to engage the students in creating their own patterns. Using the Infinite Cloner (SMART™) feature of the IWB software, the teacher first created three different shapes (for example, a red circle, a green triangle, and a blue square). The students could then drag from these shapes to make endless clones, which made it simple for the pattern creations. (This feature is known as Drag a Copy on Promethean IWBs and is a feature in almost all IWB programs.) The teacher was able to model several different patterns for students. Then, she invited students to come to the board to create their own. As the lesson progressed and students were engaged in making patterns at their desks with physical objects, student pairs continued to cycle through the IWB making their own patterns using the three shapes.

Stop and Think: Mathematics

Choose from these options to begin building a bank of IWB activities for mathematics:
- Create a self-checking IWB activity for an upcoming mathematics topic or for review of a skill already taught.
- Search online for a ready-made IWB mathematics lesson to use with students.
- Find an electronic interactive mathematics practice or review game to play with students on the IWB.
- **Challenge!** Create a series of pages or slides to use during an upcoming mathematics unit. Include an introductory activity, self-checking practice slides, story problems for students to solve, and an electronic game related to the concept or skill. (For information on how to link a Web page to an IWB page, see Chapter 6.)

Science

Much of a teacher's science instructional time might be spent engaging students in hands-on activities and experiments. Certainly, there is no substitute for having students physically manipulate objects and materials to explore a scientific concept. However, for those times when hands-on is simply not practical, virtual is the next best thing. The suggestions that follow offer simple ways to engage students in science learning through the use of an interactive whiteboard. Additionally, the websites in Appendix C provide links to interactive science-related activities for students to use online.

Life Science

- Use the IWB resource library to have students create a page of things they see, another page of things they smell, and other pages for things they hear, taste, and touch. Students can use the class ideas to create their own senses booklet.

- Use the plant and animal pictures in the IWB software database to create a food web or food chain on a blank page. Or have the pictures selected ahead of time, and have students drag them to show how they interact. Use the Pen or Typing tools to label each animal as a producer, a primary consumer, or a secondary consumer.

- Create a page to introduce a new unit. Pose a question such as *Why can a cactus live in the desert?* Link informational websites to pictures on the page. (For information on how to link websites directly to IWB pages, see Chapter 6.) View the information, and have students take notes in their science journals. The class can revisit the question and add links to the page throughout the unit.

- Create a picture- or word-sorting activity to categorize animals by phylum, class, order, family, genus, or species.

- Hook up a digital microscope to the computer to project onto the IWB. Use the microscope software and IWB tools to make observations about the images. Teachers who do not have access to a digital microscope can search online for and project virtual microscopic images of a specific object. (For information on using other software programs with an interactive whiteboard, see Chapter 6.)

- Stream videos that show how each body system works. Create an IWB page for each system with a picture and text, and have students drag the words to label each part of the system.

- Use a sequencing template to have students order the steps in a life science process, such as the life cycle of a frog or plant or the nitrogen cycle.

- Conduct a virtual dissection. Froguts, Inc. is a Bio-eLearning company that has developed realistic simulations of several dissections for use on interactive whiteboards. Students use virtual tools such as holding pins, scalpels, and scissors to work through the dissection. Visit http://www.froguts.com for more information.

Earth Science

- Create a sorting activity for students to list features of each type of rock. Or copy and paste images of examples of each type of rock onto its own slide or page (e.g., one page for sedimentary, one page for igneous, and one page for metamorphic). Then, have students identify common characteristics of each type of rock to develop background knowledge before reading about their specific features. (Learn how to include images that cannot be copied and pasted into an IWB page by using the screen shot function. See Chapter 6 for details.)

- Create a sorting activity with text and pictures for students to identify each type of fault boundary.

- Use IWB pictures and drawing tools to create a visual representation of the water cycle.

- Create an IWB page or slide with a simple table upon which to record the daily weather. At the end of the week, have students compare and discuss the data. Use IWB graphing options to chart the week's low and high temperatures.

- Complete a Venn diagram comparing the inner and outer planets.

- Create a self-checking pretest related to the sun, Earth, and the moon. Use a student response system, or have students write and display their answer (A, B, C, or D) on an individual student whiteboard. Have students retake the same quiz as an end-of-unit review before they take a summative assessment. (For information on using a Student Response System with the IWB, see Chapter 6.)

- Stream a video that explains, in kid-friendly terms, the processes of weathering and erosion. Create a write-in weathering and erosion summary page (see Figure 5.5). Or, as a class, complete a triple Venn diagram to compare the three types of physical weathering. Have students collaborate to complete the information on the interactive whiteboard.

Figure 5.5 Sample Graphic Organizer for Weathering and Erosion

Write three causes and their effects to explain weathering and erosion.

Cause	Effect

Physical Science

- Create a sorting or matching activity with words or pictures for the three states of matter.

- Create a picture- or word-sorting activity by changing state, either physical or chemical.

- Create a picture-sorting activity for students to identify objects that are and are not attracted to magnets. Have students test their predictions and then make corrections on the IWB page.

- Connect to and conduct an online interactive activity related to force and motion. BBC has a website with many simple science learning activities, including those related to physical science topics, sorted by age groups at http://www.bbc.co.uk/schools/scienceclips/index_flash.shtml.

- Stream an online interactive roller coaster-designing activity. Work as a class to create the most outrageous working roller coaster. Teachers might try the "Coaster Creator" activity from National Geographic's "The Jason Project" at http://www.jason.org/digital_library/4851.aspx.

- Investigate a Science, Technology, Engineering, and Mathematics (STEM) learning activity such as "Building Big" from PBS at http://www.pbs.org/wgbh/buildingbig/. Students can learn about the construction of large structures, participate in interactive labs and construction challenges, and explore real-world applications.

> **Stop and Think: Science**
>
> Choose from these options to begin building a bank of IWB activities for science:
>
> - Create a self-checking IWB activity for an upcoming science topic or for review of a concept already taught.
> - Search online for a ready-made IWB science lesson to use with students.
> - Find an electronic science game or activity to play with students on the IWB.
> - **Challenge!** Create a series of pages or slides to use during an upcoming science unit. Include an introductory activity, informational slides (or slides with links to informational sites; see Chapter 6), self-checking review slides, and an electronic game or activity related to the concept.

Social Studies

Many social studies teachers like to use primary source documents to support their instructional objectives. *Primary sources* are authentic materials such as letters, documents, maps, pictures, speeches, or articles that transport the reader to a specific point in time and allow him or her to make observations and draw conclusions about its historical significance. Many primary sources are available on the Internet, so their projection onto an interactive whiteboard is a natural means of displaying and discussing them with students. The teacher can highlight, circle, or otherwise note important ideas with students. This way, their review becomes a guided-learning activity, providing the instruction students need to begin to analyze social studies topics from a unique perspective.

Whether teachers use documents, documentaries, or other media, the following ideas should help enhance social studies instruction with the use of the interactive whiteboard.

Geography

- Use Google Maps™ (http://maps.google.com) to teach map skills (e.g., cardinal directions and scale). Map a path around town, use the map to find an alternate route, and calculate distances.

- Use Google Earth™ (http://www.google.com/earth/index.html) to virtually visit any place in the world, from the students' school to the Taj Mahal. Teachers can also use Google Earth to investigate various geographical features such as plains, mountains, and peninsulas from many vantage points.

- Explore an interactive drag-and-drop world geography activity such as "GeoGames" from "Reach the World" http://www.reachtheworld.org/games/geogames/index.html.

- Create a national, regional, state, or local map-labeling activity. Use IWB software to include the desired map and then include text with labels around the map. Have students drag the names of locations to the correct places on the map. Put the answers in a pulltab for self-checking.

- Create a sorting or matching activity for students to match the names of mountain ranges, major bodies of water, or other geographical features to their correct state, country, or continent.

History

- Create an IWB page or slide for students to brainstorm a list of monuments they know about or have heard about. Use the student-generated list to design and create informational slides about each monument. Create a sorting activity for students to distinguish between natural and man-made monuments.

- After learning about Native American tribes, have students complete a Venn diagram on an interactive whiteboard page to compare two tribes. They can use the Pen tools to write in the spaces, or type ideas for them to drag and drop into the correct spaces to compare the tribes.

- Create a time line on an IWB page of events related to a specific era or topic in history that the class is studying. List events around the time line by using the Text tool. Have students drag and drop the events into the correct order on the time line.

- Visit a local or national daily news publication online. Spend time at the beginning of each class period sharing one headline and article of interest with students. Discuss how this event plays an important role in history and how it affects today's society.

- Create an informational IWB slide or page about an event in history that students are studying.

- Find online and display a "This Day in History" website. Each day, share important historical events related to that date as a transition into the class period.

Civics

- Pose this thought-provoking question by typing it into a headline on a blank IWB page or slide: *Should the government require all of its citizens to vote?* Poll the class. Record the results. Then, record the students' ideas that support this notion and the ideas that refute this notion. Save the students' responses, and revisit the question and re-poll students after they have completed their civics unit. Compare the polling results.

- Create a write-in sorting activity for students to list ways people can participate in government in their community, state, and/or nation.

- Stream an online activity from iCivics.org at http://www.icivics.org. Students play games and participate in simulations around many topics related to civics education.

- Stream "The Democracy Project" from PBS at http://pbskids.org/democracy. Students can learn about the history of voting in the United States, be president for a day, and catch up with current election news.

- Search online for a copy of the text of the Declaration of Independence, the Bill of Rights, or the United States Constitution. (Or, search for the primary-source documents to display for students.) Have students read sections of the text that the teacher has strategically highlighted with the Highlighter tool. Discuss the meaning of the message. Then, have students rewrite the text in more "kid-friendly" language on a blank IWB page.

Economics

- Create a slide or page for students to sort pictures or words into two categories: goods and services.

- Create a slide or page with miscellaneous items the students would want to buy. Draw price tags on the items and include prices. Give each group of two or three students a specific amount of money to spend. Have students work collaboratively with their groups to spend their money on the items listed on the board. Discuss how each group spent its share of the cash and how they reached decisions regarding what to purchase.

- Conduct a mock stock market unit. Decide on a stock to purchase by using the Internet to research various stocks of interest. Create a page using a data entry program to track and graph the stock price over time. Add a link to check the stock's value at the start of class each day. Use a blank IWB page to calculate losses and gains at the end of each week. Maintain this data in a spreadsheet. Discuss economic factors that might be affecting the stock's price each day and each week. (For information on using and linking other software programs and websites, see Chapter 6.)

- Use clip art images, illustrations, and words to create a class concept map on a blank IWB page related to the local or national economy.
- Link to and play one of the online economics games from GameQuarium at http://www.gamequarium.com/economics.html.

> **Stop and Think: Social Studies**
>
> Choose from these options to begin building a bank of IWB activities for social studies:
> - Create a self-checking IWB activity for an upcoming social studies topic or for review of a concept already taught.
> - Search online for a ready-made IWB social studies lesson to use with students.
> - Find an electronic social studies game, activity, or simulation to play with students on the IWB.
> - **Challenge!** Create a series of pages or slides to use during an upcoming social studies unit. Include an introductory activity, informational slides (or slides with links to informational sites; see Chapter 6), self-checking review slides, and an electronic game or activity related to the concept.

Technology

Since most students in today's classrooms are "digital natives," it is easy to forget that they still need instruction related to effective and appropriate use of technology functions and features. An interactive whiteboard is a perfect tool for demonstrating these functions since the whole class can watch and learn and then turn to their own computer to practice the process. As in other content-area instruction, students benefit from watching both their teacher and their fellow classmates manipulate items on the screen to achieve the desired results. And the more practice students have with these functions, the more proficient they become with them.

Some aspects of technology that require direct instruction and guided practice include:

- Learning and applying keyboarding skills
- Inserting and positioning images, pictures, clip art, shapes, and other graphics
- Using spreadsheet and graphing software, including data entry, chart options, titles, colors, and graphics
- Editing a word-processing document, including how to change fonts, styles, sizes, and colors of text for maximum impact
- Using search engines effectively and distinguishing between reliable and unreliable Internet sources

Health and Fitness

There is a growing urgency to teach students to eat healthfully and engage in healthy lifestyle habits. Movements such as Michelle Obama's "Let's Move" campaign and the National Football League's "Play 60" campaign have brought an awareness of fitness to children and their families through public service announcements and personal challenges. These movements support local efforts to keep children eating healthfully and staying active. Many state curriculum standards include objectives related to health and safety or nutrition.

The following interactive whiteboard activities can be used to kick off a unit on health and fitness.

Nutrition

- Create a picture-sorting activity for students to identify foods that belong to various food groups.
- Create a class "Must Do" list of healthy eating habits.
- Find a grade-level-appropriate online article related to food and nutrition. Read it as a class. Use the Highlighter tool to highlight the main ideas.
- Model for students on the IWB how to keep a personal food diary. Teachers can use a weekly calendar program to list the foods they eat each day, or they can use a word processing program and simply date each entry. Then, students can record their own food intake on a personal calendar or in a journal.

Exercise

- Write or type a class pledge related to fitness at the top of an IWB page. Have each student use the Pen tool to sign the pledge and include how many hours each week he or she commits to exercise. After one week, revisit the pledge page. Have students write a summary evaluating their success at meeting their pledge.
- As a class, brainstorm a list of ways students can exercise in and out of school.
- Create a table with students' names and a space beside their names. As a morning check-in, have students record the number of minutes they exercised the night before. Add up the students' minutes. Determine the number of hours the class exercises each night and each week.

IWB Tips *from an expert*

Although most of the IWBs at our school are mounted in classrooms, we also have two boards that are mobile, on rolling stands. One of these boards is often utilized by the physical education teacher. For a recent unit on muscles and exercise, the teacher created an IWB file that allowed students to drag and drop the names of the major muscles onto a diagram of the human body. The IWB was set up as one station for the students to rotate through. As part of the IWB activity, the students also identified the major muscles utilized during the exercises at the various stations.

Healthy Lifestyle Choices

- Type a situation on a blank page that evokes a feeling or emotion. Discuss how this situation would make students feel and what they would do next. Record their ideas on the page using the Pen tool. For example, how would students feel about the following: "You are playing on the playground when a mean-looking dog wanders near you. How would this make you feel? What would you do next?"

- Create an IWB slide or page with two boxes. In one box, type one choice. In a second box, type another related choice. Examples are *candy or pizza*; *game day or movie day*; and *video games or board games*. Have students move to sit on the left or right side of the board to show which choice they would make. Do this with several choices. Discuss whether the choices were easy or difficult to make, and why.

- Have students work in groups to create and present an interactive project to the class that addresses drug-related topics. Students can make a slide-show presentation, write a story using story-making software, or create a poster using an online poster-making program such as Glogster (http://www.glogster.com). (For information on how to use other software programs with an interactive whiteboard, see Chapter 6.)

Character Development and Anti-Bullying

- Create a page or slide with two areas to type, perhaps two rectangles or a square and a circle. Title the slide with an area of the school, such as *Cafeteria*, *Front Office*, or *Playground*. Use the Pen or Typing tool to list in the first spaces examples of positive behavior in this area of the building. Type or write nonexamples in the second space on the IWB page. Complete one page or slide for each area of the school where students spend time (e.g., the bathroom, the nurse's clinic, the bus stop). Periodically review the appropriate slide as the students' behaviors warrant.

- Create situational cards on IWB pages or slides that address bullying. Read each situation as a class and then discuss how students would respond from different perspectives. For example, one card might read, "Bruce and Greg like to make fun of other students. They call them names and laugh when they make mistakes. What would you do if you were the teacher? A girl in the class? A boy in the class? The parent of one of the students being made fun of? The school principal?"

- Create an informational IWB page or slide to introduce and teach students about a positive character trait each week or each month. Include the trait, its definition, and a sorting activity for students to identify examples and nonexamples of this trait.

Other School-Site Uses

Of course, an interactive whiteboard is the perfect tool to enhance, enliven, and improve instructional practices. After all, the overall goal with any device or program in education is to increase student achievement. However, often these same instructional tools and practices reach beyond the classroom. Additional opportunities for using IWBs at the school site are offered below.

Parental Involvement

Parental involvement is an essential component to any successful school. If a school has family-involvement nights or parent workshops or otherwise involves parents in some way, consider sharing special presentations on the IWB. Just as students enjoy learning with an IWB, their parents will find it equally engaging. As mentioned in Chapter 2, an IWB is most effective in a classroom setting, so presentations that are projected on an auditorium screen would be less interactive. Teachers could still complete the presentation using IWB software and run the presentation from the computer, but all the interactive features would need to be run through the computer rather than at the board itself.

During Back-to-School Night or Open House, teachers can put their IWB to work dazzling parents and exciting students by sharing interactive projects that the class has created. Imagine a parent night in which students interact with the board and invite their parents to interact with them. This presentation is sure to be more engaging than the traditional lecture format of many presentations for parents.

IWB Tips *from an expert*

During Back-to-School Night and other family nights, many teachers take the opportunity to have students show their parents how to use the IWB. This works best if the student engages their parent in an activity that the student has previously completed. Teachers require students to practice for these interactions so that a logical series of steps is followed. During a recent Family Math Night, fifth-grade students demonstrated the many IWB games they use to reinforce instructional content. The parents were not only impressed with their children's technology skills but they learned some math as well!

Teacher Tip!

Back-to-School Night is a great opportunity to use the IWB. Prepare a "welcome" slide show for parents and share expectations, the course syllabus, schedules, pictures, student work samples, instructional programs, or any other information of importance.

Intervention and Tutoring

Intervention and before- and after-school tutoring provide additional instruction and support to students to solidify new learning. An IWB can be an effective tool in these situations. Many schools have an intervention curriculum that includes engaging, targeted, and meaningful interactive software or programs designed to fill gaps in students' content knowledge. For small-group instruction, these programs may be projected, and the group may interact collaboratively with the program to build confidence and mastery. Teachers can also project practice problems and model how to complete them through repeated guided practice.

Professional Development

Students are not the only ones engaged in learning at schools. Teachers, too, participate in professional-development sessions. Sometimes, these take place in small groups, such as when teachers participate in a professional study group or book study. Anyone who facilitates professional development sessions for colleagues can develop presentations using IWB software for this purpose. This might include linking videos, conducting book discussions, joining blogs, investigating and sharing curriculum resources, learning about instructional best practices, investigating assessment options and resources, listening to podcasts, or participating in webinars. Whether session coordinators conduct a traditional book study or use advanced-technology features, the use of an IWB can enhance any professional-development presentation by more actively involving participants.

Chapter Summary

As with any new product or process, many teachers need time to assimilate the information, see it used in situations similar to their own, and/or have time to develop their lessons to integrate the new idea or practice. Hopefully, the ideas in this chapter have sparked some meaningful ideas for teachers of any grade level or any content area. This chapter provided simple and engaging introductory, learning, and practice ideas for incorporating IWBs into instruction. The only way to start something new is to simply get started. Collaborate with other teachers who are beginning to use an IWB. Trade IWB page files to build a repertoire of interactive lessons. Try adding one new element each week (or every other week) until the many basic functions available have been discovered and utilized. Then, when ready, teachers can embark on Chapter 6, which provides suggestions for IWB integration with advanced features. Once a teacher starts teaching content with the interactive whiteboard, he or she will wonder how students have managed to learn anything thus far without it!

Reflection Questions

1. What will be the first subject area for which you will devise an interactive whiteboard activity?

2. How do you envision this activity will enhance learning for your students?

3. Which subject area will be the most challenging for you to create IWB activities? What resources (online or otherwise) can help you get started?

Chapter 6

Exploring Advanced Features of the Interactive Whiteboard

The use of an interactive whiteboard can motivate students to reach new levels in their learning. Chapter 5 explored easy-to-use, ready-made templates that are part of the IWB software to design and create interactive lessons and activities. When teachers become comfortable using their IWB software for basic functions, they can move into more complex (but not complicated) applications of the interactive-whiteboard features. By implementing advanced features of the interactive whiteboard, teachers can customize lessons and make the most of the technology. Additionally, these features allow teachers to create more meaningful lessons and activities designed specifically for the class. They allow teachers to better utilize the software resources and to add a touch of their own personalities to new lessons as well as to the lessons and activities they may have already created.

Do not fear the advanced features! Teachers can begin to stretch their IWB expertise as much as—or as little as—suits their comfort level with regard to lesson planning and instructional delivery. These advanced features will enliven lesson-plan development even more.

Creating an Interactive Game Board

Many teachers find friendly competition to be motivating for students. Whether students are earning individual or group points for a special reward, mastering basic facts to increase computation speed, or fighting for survival in a historical simulation, they are often actively engaged when competition is involved. Teacher-made electronic board games are an especially effective tool for fostering friendly learning competition. Teachers can design them to fit any content area and any topic within a content area. Students must recall facts and information or apply a process or procedure to answer questions about a topic they have been studying. However, students perceive these learning activities as simply games. Teachers can use the interactive whiteboard software to have students review important information and apply a skill in unique situations, both of which are essential steps in the learning process. Games are a fun, eventful, and spirited way to engage students with content while they "practice" learning.

To make a meaningful IWB board game for review and practice, follow the steps below. These games can take some time to develop, so plan ahead. Use the lesson or unit objectives to compose questions carefully so that they offer the right amount of rigor and assist students in meeting the standards.

Directions for Creating an Interactive Game Board

Step 1. Select a content area and topic. For example, create a board game to check students' comprehension of a class story, solve multistep mathematics problems or apply a mathematical concept, or review essential facts and information from a unit of study in science or social studies. The example in Figure 6.1 shows a board game related to a third-grade unit on animal adaptations.

Step 2. Decide how the game will be played in the class. Will it be a whole-class activity or a small-group activity? Will the class play it in its entirety or use it as a beginning-of-class review and only play for a short time, perhaps giving each player just one turn each day? Thinking about this ahead of time will help to establish the purpose of the questions and to visualize the activity's implementation in the classroom. The board game pictured in Figure 6.1 is intended to be a class review before a final assessment on this topic.

Step 3. Start with a blank IWB page or slide. Use a question-answer flip tile to create questions and check answers. These become the game-board spaces. Size the pieces to include at least 20 or so spaces on the board. Place the spaces in a logical path around the board. Be sure to lock the spaces in place so that they cannot be moved while students play the game. Each of the question tiles on the board in Figure 6.1 asks a factual question about vocabulary terms or specific animal adaptations that the students learned about during the unit.

Step 4. Choose game-board pieces for each player. If a board game for a small group is created, each student can likely have his or her own game piece. If the game will be played with the whole class, each table group of four to six students might each have its own game piece. The example in Figure 6.1 shows five animal game pieces, one for each table group of four students in a class of twenty third-graders.

Step 5. Add electronic features. Insert a digital die from the interactive-whiteboard resource library. Also, use a digital timer to limit the amount of time each student or each table group spends answering a question in order to keep the game moving. This can also be inserted on the game board from the IWB resource library.

Step 6. Establish rules and procedures. For example, what happens when a student answers a question correctly? What happens when a student answers a question incorrectly? How is the game played? What is the objective? How is the winner determined? (For example, is the objective simply to reach the end of the path, or will the class earn a different number of points for each question based on the level of difficulty? In this case, plan to keep track of the number of points each player or group has earned from turn to turn.)

Step 7. To play, have each player roll the die in turn and then move the game piece that number of spaces. Read the question on that space. After the student responds, click the space to turn it and reveal the correct answer. Whether the game piece advances or remains on the space, turn the game piece back over in case another player lands there. Type the directions and rules on the actual game board, on an introductory slide, or as a tab that can be displayed and hidden as needed.

Step 8. Try the game before launching it with students. Make sure all the questions are appropriate, the answers are accurate, and the board has adequate spaces for students to have several turns. Check all the digital additions to be sure that they function as intended.

> **Teacher Tip!**
>
> When playing an IWB game as a whole class, establish the game rules with the class before play begins. Decide whether students will have access to notes during play. Also make the expectations clear during play when groups are awaiting their turn. Decide whether group members will take turns answering the questions or if there will be just one spokesperson per group. The clearer the rules are before play begins, the fewer interruptions the class will encounter during play, allowing the game to progress in a timely manner.

Figure 6.1 IWB Board Game Related to Animal Adaptations

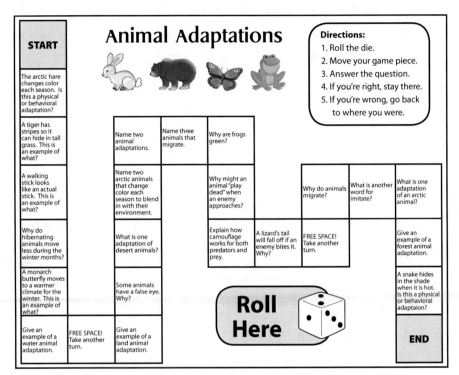

Variations on Game Boards

Game boards for the IWB can take time to develop. The following variations allow teachers to engage their students with game-like interactive activities that take less time to create.

Concentration

Teachers can use the question-answer flip tiles to create a concentration game. This is a matching game where students flip one tile, see part of one problem or answer, and then flip a second tile to see if it is a match. For example, one tile might have clues about an animal, and the matching tile could have the name of the animal. One tile might have a computation problem or quadratic equation to solve, and its match would have the answer. To create this type of game, simply leave the front of the question-answer tile blank and type the question or problem on the back only. To play, students try to match the two tiles that go together. If a match is not made, turn the tiles back over to the blank side. If a match is made, leave the spaces turned over. Students keep track of the number of matches they make. The player who makes the most matches wins.

Modifying Existing IWB Game Files

Teachers can make modifications to any IWB file containing a game they find online to better suit their classroom or subject area. For example, online searches for IWB files containing modifiable games produce results for many game templates that can be downloaded, such as variations of Jeopardy™, Whack-a-Mole™, and Connect Four™. Some online IWB games are formatted for use with a Student Response System and the links from page to page have been created, but the questions are usually customizable. These games encourage teamwork and collaboration and often require students to strategize as part of the objective. It only takes a moment to conduct an online search for an interactive whiteboard game to suit personal objectives. Simply type in the maker of the IWB and add the word *games*. Download and save the files to access at a later time to create a personalized game.

Displaying and Using Other Software Files

A teacher's computer files likely contain countless word-processing documents, slide shows, and other electronic files that teachers have created, borrowed, or discovered and used with students throughout the learning process. Additionally, many publishers provide digital resources to accompany their curricula that can be used as is or modified to better meet the needs of specific students. Using an interactive whiteboard does not mean that a teacher must purge all the great resources he or she may have accumulated. On the contrary, the IWB works in tandem with any electronic file, with or without additional equipment.

Using Existing Documents

Teachers can open any document (or link it to an IWB page; see "Linking Software Files to IWB Pages" later in this chapter) and mark on it using the IWB tools. Simply pull up a word-processing, desktop-publishing, or multimedia file on the computer. This also works for any digital image or photo—simply open and project the file onto the screen. Read it, play it, or edit it using the IWB tools and features, such as the Pen and Highlighter tools or clip art. Teachers can save changes or not, depending on the purpose of the interaction and on whether they will need to access the changes at a later date. Be cognizant of how the IWB interfaces with modifications to an original document. Some files may simply save changes by choosing the *Save* or *Save As* option. Other files may require additional steps to save changes, such as embedding the drawing features into the document. Check the IWB software manual or hunt online for a "how-to" demonstration. Or, teachers can simply use trial-and-error to find the right combination of steps to save changes. (Once discovered, keep a record of the correct steps to refer to in the future.)

Integrating Paper Copies on a Document Camera

Teachers may not have an electronic copy of some of the documents they like to use for instruction and must rely on a document camera to project its image. Most often, teachers connect their document cameras directly to the projector with a VGA cable. Unfortunately, when hooked up this way (without going through the computer), the image from the document camera is projected on the IWB, but none of the IWB tools will function on the image. However, most document cameras manufactured within the last five years can be connected to the computer via a USB cord, which allows whatever is under the document camera to be displayed in a software application on the computer. (Each manufacturer of document cameras has its own proprietary software application.) Since whatever is under the document camera is now displayed on the computer, the projected image can be marked up with the IWB tools, just like anything else that is on the computer screen. Teachers can find blogs and postings about using a document camera with an IWB by simply typing *how to use document camera with interactive whiteboard* in the online search box.

IWB Tips from an expert

When teachers discover the function of connecting their document camera to the computer via a USB cord rather than directly to the projector via the VGA (video) cable, it opens up a whole new set of options for them and their students. Now anything placed under the document camera can be viewed on the computer, and hence all the IWB functionality is available for the projected image from the document camera. One of the best uses of this functionality is displaying student writing for shared-editing purposes. Since the image of the writing is now on the computer, the editing can be done using the IWB tools rather than marking up the actual paper copy. Students are quite eager to have their work placed under the document camera for class-suggested revisions!

> **Teacher Tip!**
>
> Use the multiple Pen options to their utmost potential. When studying subjects and predicates, students might highlight subjects in blue and predicates in yellow. First graders might highlight the –*ot* in each family of –*ot* words in pink and underline or circle the onset in red pen. Teachers might show each of the steps to completing a multistep math problem (such as 452 x 86) in a unique color. Get to know the Pen and Highlighter color options. Using them can help visual learners remember important content (Jensen 2008).

Integrating Scanned Files as PDFs

The great part about an interactive whiteboard is that it works with whatever might happen to be projected onto it. This means that any document that teachers have saved as a Portable Document Format (PDF) will also work on the IWB. Word-processing documents, spreadsheets, digital images or diagrams, and student work can all be made into PDFs. This is helpful for teachers who have paper documents they want to project but lack a document camera with a USB port. Paper documents can be scanned and saved as a PDF. (This can usually be done with a printer or copy machine. Consult a colleague or IT professional for assistance with scanning documents.) Then, simply pull up the PDF and project it just like any other document.

What works for paper documents also works with scanned documents or primary source materials such as letters, paper records, receipts, pictures, brochures, menus, or maps. Anything teachers might have stored in file cabinets can be scanned, saved, projected, and utilized electronically in the classroom for instructional purposes. Students can bring in a family artifact (e.g., a letter written by a great-grandfather while serving overseas during World War II) that can now be a viable learning tool in the classroom. Once scanned and saved, it will live on digitally for years to come.

If a scanner is not available, a digital camera can be used to snap a picture of a paper document. If care is taken in positioning the camera with the document (often placing the document on the floor and standing directly above it works well) this method can work as well as scanning.

As with other electronic files, be sure to know how to save any changes that might be made using the IWB tools along with the PDF document.

Inserting Screen Shots

A *screen shot* is a picture of a computer screen that is saved as a picture or image file. Imagine that Mrs. Morgan, a sixth-grade teacher, finds a great picture of a bee magnified by a scanning electron microscope on the Internet. She wants to use the image to teach her students about the anatomy of a bee, but it is online and cannot be downloaded or saved in any usable format. Mrs. Morgan can still save the image to use with her interactive whiteboard by taking a screen shot. To take a screen shot, use the scroll bar to place the picture in the center of the computer screen. Be sure the whole picture is visible. Use an option in the IWB software to take a picture of (or "capture") the desktop and place it on an IWB page. Now, save the image as an IWB file and use it as part of a lesson.

The screen capture feature is particularly helpful when studying maps. Teachers can find a map, zoom in to enlarge it, and then take a screen shot of the map to place on a slide. This makes the map interactive. Students can trace routes to and from places in different colors, highlight important map features, and add images to embellish the map. Students can also learn about cardinal directions. Teachers can use the saved map(s) for myriad purposes as students learn about geography.

As with any image taken from the Internet, teachers should be sure to follow copyright laws and appropriately credit sources when using screen shots.

IWB Tips *from an expert*

I observed a small group of second-graders using the IWB to sequence images of the life cycle of a butterfly. The images of the different life-cycle stages were varied and engaging. I wondered where the images had come from, but the teacher was busy with a small reading group, so I made a mental note to ask her later where she got the images. Later that week, I ran into her in the hallway. When I inquired as to where she got the images, she replied, "Oh, one of my teaching partners showed me how to use the screen-capture function, and I quickly snapped them from the Internet. It was amazing—the pictures went straight from the Web page to my IWB file." She also took the time and responsibility to cite her sources on a credits page at the end of the file.

Creating Learning Activities

Interactive whiteboard software allows teachers to create interactive activities for students. But some lessons need more than just matching, sorting, or ordering practice pages. For example, Ms. Force, a fourth-grade teacher, wants to create a dynamic learning activity for the interactive whiteboard. First, she wants to review essential information from other sources. For this, she needs to access a digital word-processing document. She also wants to play an online interactive game. For this, she needs access to a particular website. Then, she wants to show students a three-minute video that she downloaded from the Internet. For this, she needs access to the multimedia file. She also wants students to complete a graphic organizer to summarize their learning from the information page and video. For this, she needs access to a graphic organizer that she has saved as a PDF file. Finally, she wants to demonstrate for students how to use a word processing program to summarize information and use text features (e.g., bolded, underlined, and italicized text) to showcase specific information. For this, she needs access to a word-processing program. All these "needs" are available through interactive-whiteboard software. Ms. Force can open text and multimedia files that have been linked directly to an IWB page and use IWB software to modify the documents and save (or not save) changes. She can link a website directly to an IWB page so that it opens with a tap on the whiteboard. And she can display other software programs and model how to use their functions. She can do all of this at the front of the room with the use of her IWB tools. All Ms. Force needs to do to make all of her electronic resources available to students is to link them to one IWB file either on one page or across several pages.

Linking Websites to IWB Pages

Teachers can pull up an online resource, whether it is a game, an informational site, or an activity page, right from the computer and project it onto the interactive whiteboard screen. In this case, the computer will be projecting "live" from the Internet. Teachers can use the IWB software to mark up online text and interact with the program, but it would still be a stand-alone activity; a Web browser would need to be opened and minimized on the computer and then maximized at the appropriate time. Instead, any website can be linked right onto an interactive whiteboard page or slide. This way, the Internet link becomes a permanent part of an IWB lesson. Teachers only need to open their IWB lesson and run through the slides. When they get to the place where they inserted the website, clicking the link opens the respective Web page. When teachers close the IWB lesson, the website stays embedded within the lesson. This is especially helpful because the website will be easily accessible for future instruction.

> **Prezi Presentations**
>
> Prezi is a cloud-based presentation-software program. Users can add images and text to an open canvas, group related ideas, and link them in a logical progression. It works a lot like slide-show software, but it allows for a nonlinear presentation of information. Interested teachers can find out more at http://prezi.com. Educators can sign up for a free basic account. This program is perfect for creating interactive lessons for students, parents, and teachers.

Linking Software Files to IWB Pages

Document files, like websites, can be linked to any IWB page by simply inserting a link to the file or by linking the file to an object that has been inserted onto the IWB page. This includes any file that may be saved on the computer, from word-processing documents to multimedia (video) files. For example, Mr. Jacobs, an eighth-grade teacher, is completing a class investigation that requires data collection from each of six lab groups. He can prepare ahead of time a spreadsheet for recording and assembling the data from each group. Then, he can link this file to an IWB lesson presentation related to the objective of the investigation. So, when he presents his IWB lesson to students, access to the spreadsheet is only a click away. At the appropriate point in the lesson, Mr. Jacobs can link to the spreadsheet file, record each group's data, save it, and then demonstrate how to use the graphing function of this software to create a chart of the class data. Once the chart is created, it can be copied and pasted back into the IWB presentation and referenced the next day to continue an analysis of the information from which students may draw conclusions.

> **Teacher Note**
>
> Some interactive-whiteboard software allows the user to import Microsoft PowerPoint™ slide shows right into the IWB software. The contents of the PowerPoint™ file can then be viewed as slides directly in the IWB file.

Linking Slides Within an IWB Lesson

The ability to navigate easily between slides within an IWB lesson is a useful function of IWB software. Imagine that Mrs. Hensley, a second-grade teacher, is putting together a comprehensive unit plan related to patriotic symbols and holidays. As she develops the IWB lesson pages for the unit, she soon realizes that not all of the slides are fitting into a linear presentation progression. What started out as a very sequential progression of information has quickly expanded into a web of facts, activities, and exploration. Mrs. Hensley finds it necessary to link slides out of order. As she creates her presentation, the IWB pages are automatically created in sequence, as in a slide show. However, interactive-whiteboard software offers the option of linking a slide to a later (or earlier) slide in the progression rather than automatically moving sequentially through the slides. Figure 6.2 shows how this might look. This IWB page is actually the third slide in a series of 10. The students' task is to match the image to the right holiday. Once they make their guesses, they can click on the symbol beside each image. This takes students to a linked page that tells about this holiday. So, when they click the link beside the tombstone, students learn about Memorial Day. When they click the link beside the American flag, students learn about the Fourth of July. Each of these informational slides is not necessarily part of the activity, but each slide is still part of the overall presentation.

Figure 6.2 IWB Page with Link to a Slide at the End of the Series

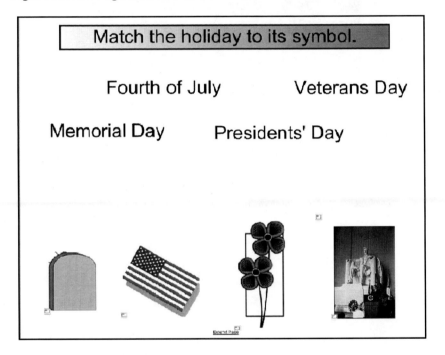

IWB Tips from an expert

Teachers and students have many options for creating digital presentations. Perhaps the most popular venue for student work is PowerPoint, but other options exist! Our third-grade teachers have recently begun having students create presentations in the IWB software. Rather than having each student create a completely separate file, the teachers have each student create one slide and then combine those into a class file or presentation. To avoid having to scroll through the document to arrive at a particular student's page, one teacher came up with the idea of creating a table of contents that linked to each student's page. So in the final presentation, each student simply clicked on his or her name and they were taken directly to their page. Much to the teacher's excitement, one of the students came up with the idea of creating links from their pages back to the table of contents.

Putting It All Together

The interactive-whiteboard software likely has many options related to how teachers can link slides, objects, files, and websites. To get started, use the following general steps. For more specific directions on how to accomplish this goal, consult a software manual, ask a colleague who may be more proficient with this particular task, or search online for video "how-to" files for a visual demonstration.

Directions for Linking Files and Websites to an IWB Page

Step 1. Create as many IWB pages or slides as needed to conduct the lesson. (See Chapter 4 for an effective lesson-planning format.) Include slides for each stage of an effective lesson.

> *"Teachers should think through how they intend to organize information. They should group information into small, meaningful segments before they start developing the digital flipcharts [IWB files]. Once they've organized the content, then they can design the flipcharts [IWB files] to complement the organization. To ensure that they don't run through the flipcharts too quickly, teachers can insert flipcharts [IWB files] that remind them to stop the presentation so students can process and analyze the new information."*
>
> —Marzano 2009, 81

Step 2. Run through the presentation from start to finish. Make notes about additional information to add that might assist students with the information and tasks presented.

Step 3. Review the notes. Link essential slides or pages, documents, multimedia clips, or websites to the page(s) where they are needed. Go to the first slide that will have a hyperlink to another slide, document, file, or website. Usually, teachers can insert a piece of clip art to act as a button for the link. Right-click on the clip art for the Add Link or Hyperlink option. Choose the type of link to add (e.g., to a slide, a file, or a website). To link to another slide, designate which slide to link to and then be sure to add a link back to the original slide. To link to a file on the computer, browse the files for the right document. To link a website, type in or copy and paste the Uniform Resource Locator (URL) into the box.

Step 4. Save changes. Then, try the links to be sure they work correctly. If a link does not work, try uninstalling and then reinstalling the link.

Another way to insert a document, file, or website is to simply choose "Add Link" right onto the blank IWB page (without the use of a clip art button). In this case, when teachers choose the file name or insert the website, this text will appear right on the page with a little button or icon to press to access it. Teachers can try linking both ways and see which way they prefer.

> **Multimedia Links**
>
> Teachers can link multimedia files in one of two ways. The first way is to stream the video "live" from the Internet each time they access the link on the IWB page. To do this, insert a link on the IWB page to a Web page. Type the URL into the appropriate space. The Web address will appear on the IWB page. Click the icon that appears to link the website with the video. Whenever the IWB lesson is projected the link will work as long as the computer has Internet access. Another option for inserting a video is to download the video and save it to a document folder or to the desktop. In this case, insert a file from the computer onto the IWB page. When students click the icon on the IWB page, the computer will open a video-viewing program to show the video.

Creating Multimedia with IWB Tools

Interactive-whiteboard software has options to include audio and video recordings that teachers synthesize themselves. This allows teachers to customize lessons for their students.

Creating and Adding Audio Recordings

IWB software has a recording option, and teachers can link audio recordings to IWB pages. Teachers can record accurate pronunciations of vocabulary words, directions for tasks to support English language learners or emergent readers, or phonemes to build phonemic awareness.

Recording sounds is as simple as clicking a button to start recording. Teachers who are using an older computer might need to add a microphone to their hardware. But most newer computers have recording mikes built right in. Locate the microphone on the computer and direct the voice into it for maximum clarity. Most IWB software has recording capability built in, but if not, teachers can use a free open-source software program for recording and editing sounds, such as Audacity®. This works on both Microsoft and Macintosh platforms. Record the words or sounds to use with an IWB page. If a teacher wants to record vocabulary terms, each word would need to be saved as its own file. Then, each recording would be linked individually to the appropriate object or word. These recordings may save as .wav files. It is better to link MP3 files to IWB images and text. To change the format of the sound file, simply use the Audacity® program to open the saved sound and then export it as an MP3 file. Once all the recordings are prepared, follow the steps outlined earlier in the chapter to insert the sound files just as you would any other hyperlink. Then, when students click on the object or word, they will hear the sound attached to it.

IWB Tips *from an expert*

At times, young students have trouble using the IWB for independent activities during centers even when the activities have been previously modeled and practiced. The solution? Provide audio directions as an optional reminder for the students. When students come to the board, give them the option of clicking on their teacher's picture, which is linked to the teacher's voice reminding students of the procedure for completing the activity.

Teachers can use linked recorded sounds to:

- Pronounce vocabulary words or phrases
- Retell stories or narrate events
- Summarize important points
- Explain directions
- Add commentaries to photos, images, and text
- Have students recite stories and poems that they authored

Video Recording an IWB Lesson

IWB software can record video of everything that happens as it happens both on the board and in the classroom. It will simultaneously record every action the teacher and his or her students make on the board during a lesson, and it will also record the audio around the board. The benefit of this advanced feature is that teachers can record and save lessons, student tutorials, and "how-to" videos. They can also record an entire lesson for use at a future date or to share online. For example, a teacher can record an entire lesson on the steps for solving mathematics problems or choosing and applying formulas. Then, the teacher can link this video to a personal website. Students can access a video file to watch a tutorial in small groups or from their computers at home. This video-recording feature is great for assuring that students who are absent do not miss a lesson. Also, when a teacher is absent, he or she can instruct the substitute to run the video file of a prerecorded lesson.

IWB Tips — *from an expert*

I walked into a kindergarten classroom to see most of the students sitting at their table groups working on printing correctly. The students had wide-lined paper and were practicing a defined set of letters, first following dotted outlines of the letters and then practicing them independently. Then, I noticed a video running on the IWB. The teacher had chosen the lined-paper background from the IWB resource library and used the video-recording feature to capture the proper formation of the letters being practiced. These short videos were then placed into the IWB file and set to loop. The students had only to look up at the IWB to be reminded of the proper form-and-stroke sequence to correctly write the letters.

Teachers can use IWB desktop video recordings to:

- Share lessons with absent students the next day
- Prepare lessons for a substitute to ensure that content will be delivered accurately
- Post lessons to a personal website for students (and parents) to access for review
- Share expertise with other educators

To record a video of a lesson, find the icon within the IWB software that allows this. Simply click the Start Recording button, and everything that happens both on the screen and aloud will record (as long as a microphone is hooked up to the computer). When finished, simply press the button to stop recording. A menu option to save the file will automatically pop up. The computer will transform the recording into a document file. Choose the location to save the file, and give it a name to identify it quickly and easily. If double-clicked, the video will open in a default media-player program. To edit or revise the recording in any way, open the media file with a media program that allows for edits and revisions. To convert the media file to a different type of media file (such as from a .wmv to an .mp4), use program-converter software. An IT professional should be able to assist with this task, if needed.

> **Teacher Tip**
>
> When video recording a lesson, as with audio recordings, be sure the computer has a working built-in or external microphone so that everything spoken records along with the actions on the screen.

Using IWB Math Tools

There are plenty of valuable online math manipulatives available that can be accessed and used to model a variety of mathematical concepts with students (see Appendix C). Additionally, most IWB software programs have math tools available. Spend some time learning about the math tools presently available within the IWB program software. Teachers who want to find out whether they can utilize additional options can visit their IWB program website and search the database for free upgrades. (For information on updating software programs, see Chapter 3.) Figure 6.3 provides a list of basic math tools and suggestions for their application. Figures 6.4 and 6.5 show examples of specific math tools.

Figure 6.3 Math Tools

Math Tool	Application
calculator	Check accuracy of manual calculations; modeling use of calculator
protractor	Measure and compare angles
ruler	Measure line lengths; draw straight lines
compass	Model how to create circles of varying radii and arcs
equation generator	Create, solve, and graph equations
thermometer	Model reading temperatures
balance scale	Model measurement of weight or concepts in algebra
dice roller, spinner, coin flipper	Discuss probability
pattern blocks	Patterning, basic shapes, fractions
tangrams	Spatial reasoning
clock	Telling time; elapsed time
algebra tiles	Solving equations

Figure 6.4 Thermometer

Figure 6.5 Protractor

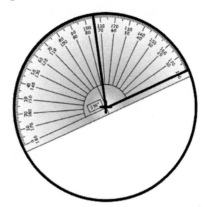

Some IWB software will also interface with other math-related technology, such as a Texas Instruments™ graphing calculator. This is a valuable feature for advanced mathematics and their applications, including calculus, statistics, and trigonometry. Teachers who are interested in learning more about these types of advanced math tools to use with an IWB can conduct an online search specific to the hardware they have, search the website of the manufacturer of their IWB, or ask colleagues or an IT professional for support.

Importing Files for the Student Response System

One of the many benefits of using interactive-whiteboard technology is that teachers can integrate the use of a Student Response System (SRS). When used appropriately, it plays a vital role in student assessment. Teachers can opt to create quizzes and tests right in the interactive software program they have. Or they can usually import quizzes and tests that are already saved as another program file, such as a word-processing program, a slide-show program, or even PDFs.

Advantages of Using a Student Response System

- Manage, track, and evaluate student progress with the curriculum
- Manage, track, and evaluate class progress with the curriculum
- Create interactive and engaging assessments
- Immediately and easily check students' understanding of the day's content
- Provide immediate feedback to students regarding correct and incorrect answers

In addition to being able to use the IWB software along with a student response system, educational websites such as BrainPOP offer lessons and assessments that integrate with IWB software and student response systems.

Earlier in this chapter, teachers learned how to link sounds to IWB slides. This feature is also available when designing and creating quizzes and tests for use with a Student Response System. Try adding applause or a cheerful "Yippee!" to correct answers, or buzzers or an "Aw" to incorrect answers. Teachers can also import images such as clapping hands or even their own smiling visage into the quiz pages to identify the correct answers. However, Marzano cautions, "When using reinforcing features like virtual applause, teachers should make sure that students focus on *why* an answer is correct or incorrect. Although these features can produce high engagement and certainly enliven the atmosphere in a classroom, they can also be distracting if used without a clear focus on essential content" (2009, 82).

IWB Tips from an expert

The third-grade teachers had been using the SRS successfully for over a year. They came to me asking for additional ideas on how to engage the students with the hardware. I had recently been experimenting with combining the traditional SRS scenario (the students answering questions posed by the teacher) with more student-centered IWB activities. So we sat down together and designed a math activity that allowed students to interact with the IWB and to respond with the clickers. The IWB activity contained a slide that asked students to drag cats into a circle. There were both brown and white cats, and students were to drag cats to the circle so that three-fifths of the cats were brown. After a student volunteer completed this, the teacher asked students to press *Yes* if they agreed with the solution and *No* if they disagreed. By viewing the results, the class could see how many students were correct. Even though students who volunteer for this type of activity know they might make a mistake in front of their peers, most are eager to participate! This scenario is currently evolving at other grade levels. It involves students in peer review and provides the teacher with a unique opportunity to adjust instruction based on student responses.

Chapter Summary

Frequently, teachers reflect on their lessons after they have conducted them. *What went well? What would I change? Was it effective enough to help all students learn the content and master the objectives?* Each time we think of a way to improve a lesson, we should remind ourselves that the features an IWB has to offer can help us modify the lesson to be more complete and more effective. Features such as linking multimedia files and websites and recording and linking sound really help a lesson become fluid and cohesive. Everything the teacher needs for any particular lesson may be added, linked, or otherwise embedded on the IWB pages for easy access. This reduces downtime and maximizes instructional learning time for students.

Reflection Questions

1. Of the IWB advanced applications presented in this chapter, which will be the most beneficial for your classroom?

2. How can you integrate the IWB advanced applications shared in this chapter with the lessons you already have for use in your classroom?

3. How do you plan to use one or more IWB advanced features in your classroom?

Chapter 7

Differentiating Instruction with Interactive Whiteboards

Highly effective teachers masterfully individualize instruction rather than rely on a "one-size-fits-all" program or curriculum. They know their students' learning styles, interests, and readiness levels. They understand that differentiation "encompasses what is taught, how it is taught, and the products students create to show what they have learned" (Conklin 2010, 19). These teachers see themselves as "organizers of learning opportunities" (Tomlinson 2001, 16). They craft lessons that optimize learning for each and every student.

Differentiating instruction is multifaceted. It involves varying the *content* that is taught, the *process* of delivering that content, the *products* that students are expected to create that demonstrate their learning, and the *learning environments* in which learning takes place. The use of an interactive whiteboard can help teachers differentiate instruction for all learners.

> "Interactive whiteboards provide an extraordinary opportunity to create classroom environments where students with different learning styles can engage and learn from each other."
>
> —Teich 2009

Differentiating Process for Learning Styles

Most people have a preferred learning style. Someone might say, "I have to do it to understand it" or "I know that the document I am looking for is on bright-yellow paper" or "I remember when the speaker mentioned something about note taking." These statements give hints about a person's preferred learning style. There are many theories on learning styles. Kolb (1984) identified experience as the primary source for learning and development. His model has four stages in the cycle of learning: concrete experience, reflective experience, abstract conceptualization, and active experimentation. Honey and Mumford (1992) identified four main learning-style preferences: activists, reflectors, theorists, and pragmatists. Commonly in education, teachers focus on Fleming's three learning styles: *visual*, *auditory*, and *kinesthetic* (Leite, Svinicki, and Shi 2010). (Fleming [2012] has included a fourth style, *reading/writing*, in his VARK—Visual, Aural, Reading/Writing, Kinesthetic—model.) Some teachers have adopted Gardner's seven intelligences, which include visual-spatial, auditory-musical, kinesthetic-physical, linguistic, logical-mathematical, interpersonal, and intrapersonal (1993). This section explores how the use of an IWB supports visual, auditory, and kinesthetic learning styles.

> **Great Idea!**
>
> Teachers can take a learning-style inventory for themselves or have their students take one to find out their preferred learning styles. Go to a favorite search engine. Type in *learning styles inventory* or *learning styles test*. Teachers can choose one that looks suitable and appropriate and get ready to learn more about themselves and/or their students.

Visual Learners

Visual learners are keen observers. They take written notes and they may doodle. They may like presentations that are on colorful backgrounds or handouts that are printed on colored paper. They are instantly drawn to images, illustrations, charts, or other visual representations. Visual learners can clearly picture an event that is described to them orally. As teachers find, create, and develop IWB activities, they can consider the use of color and images as they pertain to the lesson and use suitable slides or pages with the visual learner in mind. IWB slides can have colored backgrounds. Teachers can add images available through the IWB software, or they can pull in pictures, clip art, or videos from other sources. Some content may be best illustrated using charts or graphs, which can also be included as part of a complete IWB lesson. A word of caution: teachers should not overload IWB slides with countless visuals. Too many images may cause confusion or distract students from the content. It is better to use one powerful visual than cram a slide with less purposeful images.

Auditory Learners

Auditory learners like to hear information. These students might seem to be off-task, but when teachers call on them, they produce an acceptable answer. They might hum, sing, or make repetitive noises. They like to read aloud and talk through problems, and they do well on oral tests. Songs and mnemonic devices are powerful instructional strategies for auditory learners. Many of the interactive features of a whiteboard provide auditory feedback (sounds) for correct and incorrect answers (or the teacher can add these in, if desired—see Chapter 6). This is a bonus for auditory learners, since they will respond positively to immediate auditory feedback. Likewise, many interactive websites include music, oral directions, and various sound effects to cue students as they progress through the activities.

> One advanced feature of interactive whiteboards is the ability to record video and audio of an entire lesson. This is particularly useful for visual and auditory learners. They can follow along with the visual presentation while listening to the lesson. For information about recording an IWB lesson, see Chapter 6.

Kinesthetic Learners

Kinesthetic learners are movers and shakers. They like movement activities, dancing, and manipulating objects, and they may stand rather than sit at their seats. They remember lessons that involve activity or demonstrations. They might talk with their hands or move their feet a lot when seated. If offered a choice, they would rather jump into a task than rely on written or verbal directions. Hands-on is the name of the game for kinesthetic learners. The IWB is the ideal instructional tool for kinesthetic learners. The main purpose of using an IWB is to increase student engagement through activity.

In order for this to happen, students must be physically interacting with the images on the board. Their actions make the activity work. This activity leads to greater retention of skills and information and therefore greater learning for kinesthetic learners. The use of a student response system also taps into the kinesthetic learning style. Rather than responding to questions orally or in writing, the use of the SRS allows students to manipulate an object and push buttons to secure their answer. It may seem trivial, but this small shift in assessment delivery can make a big difference for kinesthetic learners. Additionally, students just beginning to write can use the board to trace letters with their fingers. As Solvie states, "Writing with fingers [allows] the children to feel the shapes of words they outline, feel and see letter components that create sounds they utter, and experience a true 'hands-on' approach to creating and erasing text" (2004, under "The Digital Whiteboard and How It Works").

Differentiating for Students' Interests

One student likes camping. One student likes fishing. Another likes rocks. Five students like soccer. Three others like dance. Most enjoy video games. Classrooms are filled with students with varying backgrounds, experiences, and preferences. Incorporating students' interests in lessons can sometimes help grab their attention, thus leading to an increased level of engagement and improved learning. Once a teacher knows his or her students' interests, lessons can be developed to capitalize on those preferences. For example, if providing a problem-of-the-day in mathematics class, the teacher can modify a published problem or create one to include something of interest to the students. Or if revising sentences as a daily oral-language activity, the teacher can include objects or situations that interest students.

IWB Tips *from an expert*

A fourth-grade teacher was having trouble engaging a student in mathematical problem solving. Specifically, this student was not a strong reader and was not motivated to read word problems. She decided to display problems on the IWB that centered on baseball, since this particular student loved the sport, and included visuals she found on the Internet (e.g., photos of his favorite players and team). The teacher said that in the two days since she had introduced the problems for the first time, the student had asked her several times when he could work on his "baseball math" some more.

Identifying Students' Interests

The tips below can help teachers identify students' interests. Keep notes on information gathered about students' interests and review them as needed.

- **Talk to students.** Hold one-on-one conferences to get to know students at the start of the year, and confer with them individually throughout the year.

- **Observe students.** Listen to the conversations they have with their peers. Note the types of books they choose to read.

- **Have students respond in writing** to a prompt that allows them to share personal stories, such as a narrative prompt related to their best and worst day.

- **Invite students to bring in their favorite family photos**, and use them to prompt a writing activity related to family events.

- **Have students complete surveys** about their preferences. Consider using the student response system to survey students. Using the SRS allows for results to be easily displayed and printed; however, answer choices are limited to the multiple-choice options provided by the teacher.

Students' interests often fall in line with their learning style or Gardner's multiple intelligences. A student who enjoys sports is likely a kinesthetic learner. A talented writer is likely a visual learner or has a high linguistic intelligence (or both). When teachers plan instruction with their students' interests in mind, they can broaden the scope of the information, tap into students' curiosities, and build on prior knowledge.

Differentiating Product

Offering students choices in how they demonstrate their learning is an excellent way to differentiate for students' interests. Different ways that students can demonstrate learning through the incorporation of an IWB include:

- Creating individual presentations
- Recording and sharing a music video
- Acting out a play and using the whiteboard as the background
- Leading a virtual field trip
- Creating puzzles or activities for other students to complete

Differentiating Content for Students' Readiness Levels

Just as learning styles and interests vary among students in a classroom, so do students' readiness levels. Some students arrive at school ready to build on a solid foundation of background knowledge, while others have significant gaps in certain skills or concepts. Still other students will immediately be ready to advance and extend their knowledge beyond grade-level standards.

It is important for teachers to keep in mind that students' readiness levels may vary across content areas or even across concepts within a content area. For example, a third grader may struggle with multi-digit addition but have a firm grasp of geometry and spatial reasoning. As mentioned earlier, differentiation for students should be fluid and flexible.

Small-Group Instruction

One effective strategy for differentiating instruction is through small-group instruction. This is where a teacher divides his or her class into groups of learners based on readiness levels, interests, or learning styles. For example, Mrs. Wu might identify eight students who need to build conceptual understanding of subtraction with regrouping. She organizes her math block to allow time for small-group instruction with these students. Or, Mr. Ramirez might know that three of his students read and comprehend text two grade levels above the majority of the class. During social studies instruction, he sets aside time to meet with them to provide differentiated text—that is, text that shares the same content as the rest of the class but is written at a higher readability level—and pose higher-level questions on the subject matter. Teachers might also group students heterogeneously or homogeneously by learning style to complete group projects. Also, allowing students to select their own groups based on mutual interests can be highly motivating for them. When differentiating the learning environment, teachers should consider the unique instructional needs of their students.

> **Did You Know?**
>
> Shell Education provides curriculum and resources with texts at different readability levels for common content-area topics in mathematics, science, and social studies.

Managing small-group instruction can be very challenging for teachers. Figure 7.1 illustrates how a small-group differentiated-instructional block might look in both a 45-minute class period and in a 90-minute class period. Based on the time allotments throughout the day, individual teachers can use the models to help organize a schedule suitable to their own unique situations. In the 45-minute model, the teacher splits the class time equally between whole-group instruction and small-group instruction/independent work, leaving a small amount of time for an end-of-class review or wrap-up. This means that the teacher will be able to meet with only one group each day. In the 90-minute model, the teacher splits the class time into equal small-group instructional blocks. In this model, the teacher is able to work with up to three groups each day. It is important that students working independently or in centers during small-group time have enough tasks to engage them until their group is called. This might take the form of independent practice, a short reading or writing assignment, instructional games, or an independent or group project. Providing sufficient tasks at the appropriate level of challenge will ensure that the teacher has uninterrupted time with the group he or she is working with at the interactive whiteboard to support students with mastery of the lesson's objectives.

Figure 7.1 provides sample schedules for small-group instruction; however, small-group instruction does not typically follow the same routine each day. One group might only need 10 to 15 minutes with the teacher, while another might need 20 to 30 minutes. Teachers should use their best judgment when organizing their small-group schedules. Also, when they cannot meet with every group every day, they *should* schedule a time every day to meet with their most at-risk students, as short as this time might be, to be sure they are successful with the day's objectives and that they are practicing work correctly.

Figure 7.1 Sample Differentiated Instruction Schedules

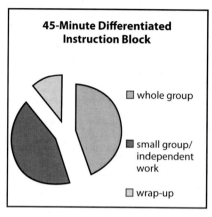
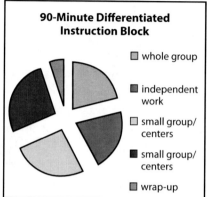

When managing small groups, be sure to do the following:

- **Set clear expectations** for small-group time. Model and practice what small-group time looks like before pulling students into small groups.

- **Provide appropriate activities** for students who remain at their seats. These activities should adequately engage students for the length of time necessary for the teacher to complete small-group work.

- **Establish a process** for students to ask questions and receive clarification should they not understand something during independent or center work time.

- **Be sure students know what they can and can't do** should they finish all their work before small-group instructional time ends.

What are the other students doing while the teacher is working with a small group of students? These ideas might help.

- Completing independent work
- Completing independent or group projects
- Engaging in a center activity
- Playing an instructional game with one or two other students
- Completing an independent writing project
- Using classroom computers for instructional support or research
- Quietly reading a book of his or her choice

Once the small-group instructional needs of students have been established, one strategy for differentiating instruction within the small group is to provide content that has been modified to meet students at their instructional levels. The teacher can thus use the interactive whiteboard to guide instruction in the needed skill areas. In the case of Mrs. Wu, she might use virtual manipulatives to reinforce the concept of regrouping. Mr. Ramirez might pull up a text selection related to the content he is teaching at a suitable readability level for the students he will work with. Once projected, he and his students can use the Highlighter and Pen tools to analyze the text and/or complete a tiered graphic organizer.

> **Recap: Differentiating Content through Small-Group Instruction**
>
> Teachers can use the IWB to differentiate content in small groups by:
>
> - Displaying and analyzing text that is below, on, or above grade level
> - Completing tiered graphic organizers or other tiered templates
> - Providing scaffolded practice by using the Revealer (screen shade) to provide hints or clues toward a solution or correct answer
> - Reteaching mathematical skills or concepts using virtual manipulatives
> - Providing additional images or picture support for texts

Differentiating Instruction for Students' Background Knowledge and Experiences

An interactive whiteboard can help teachers bring experiences to the classroom. This is particularly helpful when beginning a new unit related to a concept with which students have little or no prior knowledge. For example, when students begin learning about animal adaptations, they will be able to apply their learning much more widely if they have firsthand experiences with many animals. Unfortunately, with educational budget cuts chipping away at activities such as field trips, many students may go their whole lifetimes without seeing a snake up close or observing an elephant eating. Of course, providing firsthand experiences is always best for building students' background knowledge. However, today, almost any experience is virtually available. If an actual field trip to a zoo is not an option, a virtual field trip to a local or national zoo or simply projecting pictures of various animals for students to observe and discuss will broaden students' understanding and application of concepts.

Teachers might conduct knowledge surveys prior to beginning a new unit to determine the types of experiences their students bring to class. In the animal adaptation example, a teacher can simply have his or her students brainstorm a list of all the animals they can think of in one-minute. Once collected, the teacher can gauge whether students have had prior experiences with domestic animals, wild animals, reptiles, insects, etc. The variations in the lists will give the teacher some general understanding of his or her students' knowledge of animals. Students who list only common domestic animals, such as *dog*, *cat*, or *goldfish*, have much more limited knowledge of animals than students who list *tigers*, *giraffes*, *penguins*, and *sharks*. Once the teacher has this information, he or she may design and create IWB slides to expand students' knowledge and apply the concept of adaptations to a greater variety of animals. Lessons might include short video clips of animals in action or animals in their habitats, or pictures of more obscure animals such as the porcupine or praying mantis. Students can also use the IWB tools to circle the adaptations they identify or to summarize information about each animal. These lessons may be conducted either with the whole group or in small groups based on the feedback the teacher received from the knowledge survey.

Aside from interactive videos and pictures, teachers can also conduct prelearning activities to set the stage for future learning objectives. In reading, this might be learning about another culture or a foreign country to build background before reading a story that takes place in another country or includes characters from a different culture. In mathematics, this might include displaying a slide with a multitude of objects to count to discuss the idea of skip-counting. In science, this might be an interactive video of Earth rotating to introduce the concept of day and night. In social studies, this might include displaying a flag and having students make observations about it before learning facts about it. These simple activities may not seem like they address the idea of differentiated instruction, but when a teacher uses his or her students' prior experiences as the starting point to develop further experiences, the teacher is indeed differentiating instruction based on his or her students' background knowledge.

Recap: Building Background Experiences

Teachers can differentiate instruction with an IWB to build background experiences by:

- Taking students on a virtual field trip
- Participating in an interactive game or activity
- Showing a video and recording facts about it
- Sorting objects into categories
- Showing a picture students can use to make observations about a topic

Using an IWB in Special Education

Special education includes students with a wide range of cognitive, academic, and behavioral challenges. If a student has been identified as having special needs, he or she has an Individualized Education Program (IEP). An IEP sets specific learning goals that the student is expected to master within a set time frame. Since each student's plan is unique, general education teachers should spend time learning the goals established for their students by the IEP committee. Often, a special education teacher writes these goals. General education teachers can use feedback from the special education teacher to help plan and organize suitable IWB activities in the general education classroom that equally involve the special education students and general education students. Special education students' participation in as many general education activities as possible helps foster their self-esteem and builds their foundational skills and knowledge. These are the basis of any student's educational plan regardless of special skill considerations. Since the population of the special education classroom is usually lower than the population in the general education classroom, students have more opportunity to interact with the board, thus providing a means to better capture and maintain students' attention.

Within the special education classroom setting, the teacher can display and make use of any number of interactive learning tools, or "controlled materials" (Bender 2008, 97). This includes an interactive dictionary to build vocabulary and virtual manipulatives to practice math problems. According to Bender, the use of graphic organizers is a proven strategy to help special education students learn content better. The IWB offers students the chance to complete graphic organizers in a kinesthetic way with the support of a small-group setting. Over time and with continued support, students may arrive at the point where they can begin to complete partial organizers and even a whole organizer themselves. The use of the interactive whiteboard assists with this transition from supported to independent learner.

IWB Tips *from an expert*

Special education students at our school benefit from participating in kinesthetic activities at the IWB. The special education teacher is able to collaborate with the general education teacher so the content used to address the IEP goals aligns with the content being taught in the classroom. Recently, our fourth-grade classes were doing a unit on American Indians by region, and one of the special education students had an auditory IEP goal of being able to follow simple one-step directions. The special education teacher created a matrix that allowed the student to drag American Indian items (specific foods, clothing, shelter, etc.) into the proper category. So while the student was standing at the IWB, the teacher gave specific auditory directions such as "Drag the yellow corn into the food category." This was an engaging activity for the student, and it provided immediate visual feedback for the teacher.

As mentioned in the previous section, the use of an IWB attends to all students' learning styles. Part of addressing special education students' IEPs might include providing activities that meet the students' visual, auditory, or kinesthetic learning styles. The use of an IWB is a natural part of this process. Teachers can individualize lessons to include more visuals, more audio features, or more interactivity, depending on the needs of the special education students.

Special education students generally take longer than their peers to master skills. Therefore, they need repeated direct and guided instruction as part of the learning process. A general education or special education teacher can use the interactive whiteboard to provide the additional practice necessary to meet a wide range of skill needs among special education students. Within the general education classroom, this might take the form of a learning center at the IWB or as a small-group guided lesson at the IWB. Within the special education classroom, this might be a slide-a-day of review questions, matching or sorting activities, interactive games, or review problems. Regardless of the setting, the use of an interactive whiteboard is a valuable component of any classroom that includes special education students.

Using an IWB with English Language Learners

Many of the same differentiation strategies that apply to struggling or special education students also apply to English Language Learners (ELLs). Hollie (2011, 23) explains that the teacher's knowledge of and attendance to cultural and linguistic differences among ELL students is referred to as "culturally and linguistically responsive" teaching, or CLR. Hollie states that "[m]etaphorically, CLR is the opposite of the sink-or-swim approach to teaching and learning in traditional schools. CLR means that teachers jump into the pool with the learners, guide them with appropriate instruction, scaffold as necessary, and provide for independence when they are ready" (2011, 23). The teacher can personalize lessons and IWB pages to meet students where they are academically as well as culturally, particularly in the area of literacy.

> "Because interactive whiteboards speak to the multiple senses of sight, sound and touch, they help reinforce topics and create a compelling focal point in the classroom. Teachers can use the boards to build in informational redundancies, for example, by bringing up images or diagrams during a lesson that provide additional reference material, thereby benefiting all students, and in particular those with learning and behavioral challenges. These strategies also help ESL students by providing additional context for discussions and lessons."
>
> SMART™ 2009a, 7

A teacher's use of both fiction and nonfiction text is essential to help ELL students achieve in all subject areas. As mentioned previously, the teacher can project onto the IWB, review, and summarize text written at a simpler readability level while other students read on-grade-level text. This guided instruction using simpler vernacular (but with the same theme or content) will allow English language learners to pause more frequently to think about what they are reading, identify unfamiliar words for clarification, and discuss confusing parts with their peers. Additionally, many online texts have a read-aloud feature, which allows ELLs to hear the story or text before attempting to tackle it on their own. The classroom teacher can design and develop mini-lessons using IWB software to review complex concepts, practice using essential vocabulary terms, and pull in outside resources (including real-life pictures) to support students with their learning. Within these mini-lessons, teachers of ELL students can use any number of effective literacy strategies, such as guided reading, completing graphic organizers, or reciprocal teaching to help students learn otherwise challenging content.

IWB Tips from an expert

IWB activities can be used to both introduce and reinforce concepts for English language learners. On a recent visit to one ELL teacher's classroom, she was reviewing pronouns with third-grade students. The students were seated in front of the IWB, with the teacher standing a bit off to the side. She was asking students up to the board to sort pronouns into three categories: singular, plural, or both. A student would come up to the board, drag the pronoun into the correct category, and then orally use the pronoun in a sentence. Because the activity was done in a visual format in front of the other students, it provided the opportunity for peer assistance and review. Every student was eager for a turn at the board to show what they knew about pronouns!

Genesee et al. (2006) assert that English language learners generally learn conversational English within three years. But, as Collier (1987) notes, these same students need seven or more years to learn academic language. So, although ELLs may seem to be proficient English speakers because of their conversational skills, they may struggle academically because of a lack of academic English language acquisition. In fact, Folse (2005) reports that as students advance through their course work and English language acquisition, their major obstacle to learning is vocabulary. Therefore, direct instruction with vocabulary is one strategy from which ELLs benefit greatly. The advantage to using an IWB to support vocabulary instruction is that it can be used to help students contextually and conceptually understand new words. A student's textbook might include definitions of key terms, but an actual photograph can make a concept so much more clear. As teachers develop vocabulary lessons for their ELL students, they can pull in action photos or true-to-life pictures of objects. These may be sorted and grouped according to their characteristics, which encourages students to discuss and analyze their similarities and differences. Teachers can also develop slides to identify and match words with similar word parts, or sort words by subject area. Figure 7.2 shows a vocabulary lesson in which English language learners are instructed to sort words related to the industrial revolution into two categories: words that are examples of inventions and words that are related to manufacturing. Another strategy for developing and expanding the vocabulary of English language learners is to have them create and maintain a personal thesaurus. As students learn new content-area vocabulary, they can build on their current knowledge by listing words related to the new content-area word. For example, when learning about percentages in math, students might list real-world examples to describe when they might hear or use the term *percent* (see Figure 7.3). This may be modeled by the teacher at the IWB by listing related words as they are shared by the students.

Figure 7.2 Sample Vocabulary Sorting Activity for English Language Learners

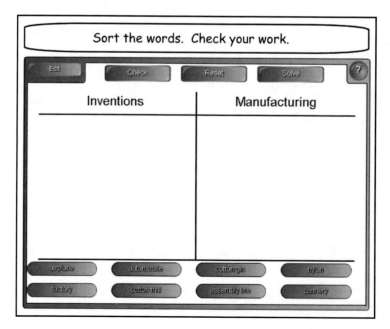

Figure 7.3 Sample Student Thesaurus Entry

Topic: Parts of a Whole

Term: percent

Related Words: per one hundred; circle graph; discounted price; sales tax; daily recommended nutrition values; grams of fat; interest on a bank account

Illustrations:

 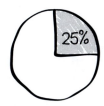

Another research-based strategy for teaching ELLs is called Total Physical Response, or TPR, a language-movement approach to learning a second language developed by Dr. James A. Asher (2000). With this method, teachers engage students' bodies in performing an action that is associated with a word or concept. For example, with beginning language-acquisition-level students, the teacher might give simple commands such as *stand up, walk to the board*, or *turn out the lights*. The students would then perform these actions. As students advance through their English language acquisition, this same technique can be used to develop students' understanding of more complex language, such as developing hand motions to demonstrate *divergent, convergent*, and *transform boundaries* or to act out the idea of *secession*. The use of an interactive whiteboard as an integral part of the classroom routine provides students with many opportunities to practice this method of TPR since they are constantly responding to their teacher's commands at the board. And the teacher can have students label IWB clip art and images to help them learn advanced vocabulary related to specific topics. When using real-life pictures and images on the IWB to help support instruction, teachers can engage students wholly by having them listen to and then respond to a command as it relates to the instructional objective. For example, to understand a character's emotions during a particular part of a story, students can act out the emotions. The teacher can take digital pictures of the students' expressions. Then, the students can use their own visages to create a storyboard using IWB slides to illustrate and label how the character's emotions change throughout the story. The students have the opportunity to comprehend and justify the character's actions and emotions, and they also develop their own personal vocabulary skills.

Accelerated Learning Opportunities with an IWB

Differentiated instruction also applies to students who need additional challenges, extensions, and acceleration in specific content areas. The use of an interactive whiteboard provides an appropriate forum for accelerated learning.

One method of acceleration is providing opportunities for students to complete independent projects. These may take any form (written, oral, or project-based), and they typically ask students to include specific criteria. With this method of acceleration, students can use the IWB to project and share their independently completed project with the class. They can include elements of interaction to keep their peers involved. And when recorded, it becomes a valuable addition to the student's learning portfolio.

Advanced students can work to bridge the connection between what Grant Wiggins and Jay McTighe refer to as "enduring understandings" and information that is "worth knowing" (1998, 10). *Enduring understandings* are the big ideas or most important understandings. They go beyond basic details and allow students to apply information in novel situations. In essence, they are the outcomes students reach as they become well-informed, productive citizens. Information that is *worth knowing* is just that: it is the topics, skills, and resources that students encounter as they assemble ideas to reach enduring understandings. As much as some teachers might like to focus their instruction exclusively on enduring understandings, they probably find themselves more frequently addressing the important facts, skills, and information related to any particular subject area's standards. Advanced students can extend basic and important content, thus demonstrating how these ideas apply in the world around them.

Options for accelerating learning include having students:

- Conduct research related to a topic and create an interactive presentation to report findings

- Use current events or sports statistics from the newspaper to create an interactive demonstration related to how players' averages are calculated

- Record audio and/or video of an interview with someone in the local community and then create an interactive presentation that incorporates the recording

- Create an interactive time line related to historical events

Chapter Summary

Differentiating instruction might seem like a daunting, insurmountable task. Teachers have so many options as to how they might go about providing suitable lessons for all the different learners in their classrooms. Fortunately, the use of an interactive whiteboard can ease the complexity and enormity of this task. An IWB naturally engages visual, auditory, and kinesthetic learners. It is a useful tool to build background knowledge. Since lessons can be individualized, the teacher can include elements related to students' interests and experiences. Its versatility makes the IWB a viable and essential tool for special education students and English language learners. An interactive whiteboard can also act as a vehicle for advanced students to extend learning beyond facts and information. All students may develop enduring understandings with the use of interactive whiteboards. This leads to better-informed and prepared citizens capable of independent thought.

Reflection Questions

1. In what ways has your thinking changed regarding the use of an interactive whiteboard to differentiate instruction?

2. How do your IWB lessons support visual learners? Auditory learners? Kinesthetic learners?

3. Which type of learner are most of your IWB lessons geared toward? How can you adjust lessons to meet the needs of students with other learning styles?

4. Think about an upcoming challenging topic or assignment. How can you develop an IWB lesson or activity to support English language learners as they learn about this topic or tackle this assignment?

Afterword

In classrooms around the world, interactive whiteboards are finding their place in the instructional arena. Teachers and students are leveraging the technology to increase learning and to bring interactivity, engagement, and enjoyment to teaching. And if you were not part of this movement before reading this book, you are now most likely well on your way.

Along with the research presented throughout this book backing the benefits of IWB use in schools, my own anecdotal experience has shown me there is a definite place for IWBs in the classroom. However, pedagogically sound teaching does not happen automatically when the IWB arrives in the classroom; throughout this book, Kathleen Kopp offers many tips and ideas to help bring quality teaching to this technology. As I have helped the teachers in my own school along this journey over the past four years, I have also made several important discoveries:

- It is crucial to connect with colleagues that also have the technology. Exchange ideas. Share discoveries. Make curricular connections together. In my school, we have the opportunity to share IWB tips and lessons in a formal setting during weekly staff meetings. These short (five to ten minute) sharing experiences allow us, as a staff, to build on each other's knowledge. If you can build this type of professional development into your school culture, you will not regret it!

- Understand that you are not going to be an advanced IWB user overnight. For most of the teachers I have worked with, it is a journey of two years or more before the IWB is cleanly integrated into each teaching day. Try not to beat yourself up because you got frustrated during that lesson yesterday when you couldn't get the IWB to do what you wanted. It will be easier the next time you try. Take a day off from your board if the frustration level gets too high.

- Be willing to take risks. I've seen the most growth from teachers who stretch themselves beyond their comfort zones. Try something new—maybe an idea from Chapter 6, *Exploring Advanced Features of the Interactive Whiteboard*. Create an interactive game board. The great thing about these game boards is that once you have created them, you will have them forever. Make sure to share them with fellow teachers, and they will probably return the favor.

In reading this book, I know you have gained both ideas and confidence to either embark on your IWB journey or take it to the next level. Along with your own growth, you will probably also notice a difference in your students as you integrate your interactive whiteboard more often to support your curriculum. They will be engaged and motivated, especially as they become more involved in interacting with the board. As a result, your students may begin giving you suggestions on how to enhance instructional delivery with the IWB. That, for me, is the *pièce de résistance*—when students not only embrace the technology, but also empower their own learning.

—Eric LeMoine

Appendix A

SMART Notebook™ How-to Guide

Advancing Pages

1. When in slide show view on the interactive whiteboard, press the forward arrow from the toolbar.

2. In full-screen view, press the forward arrow on the floating toolbar.

3. If you want to move to the previous page, press the backward arrow.

4. To return to the home page menu, press the house icon at the top of the page.

1.    2.    4.

SMART Notebook™ How-to Guide *(cont.)*

Saving a File

1. When viewing a file on a computer, select **File** from the menu across the top of the page.

2. Then select *Save*.

3. When viewing the file on an interactive whiteboard, select the Cursor tool from the toolbar.

4. Then press the *Save* icon on the toolbar.

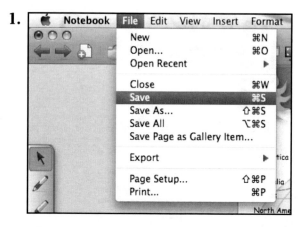

SMART Notebook™ How-to Guide *(cont.)*

Dragging Objects or Text

1. Select the Cursor tool from the toolbar.

2. Press on the desired object or piece of text.

3. Without lifting your finger, drag the object or text to the desired location.

1.    2.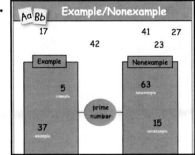

Using the Eraser

1. Select the Eraser tool from the toolbar.

2. Choose the width of the eraser by pressing the desired box with your finger.

3. Pick up the Eraser tool from the shelf on the interactive whiteboard. Use it like a regular eraser to delete the desired text or drawings. *Note:* The eraser will only remove information recorded with the Pen tool.

1. 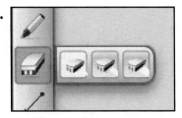   3.

183

SMART Notebook™ How-to Guide *(cont.)*

Using the Highlighting Tool

1. Select the Pen tool from the toolbar.

2. Select either the yellow highlighter or the green highlighter from the menu by pressing the desired box with your finger.

3. Highlight desired text by dragging the pen over the text.

3.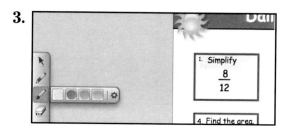

Using the Pen tool

1. Select the Pen tool from the toolbar.

2. Select a color or style from the menu by pressing the desired box with your finger.

3. Write or draw using the pen.

3.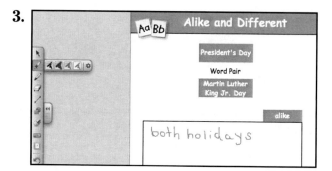

SMART Notebook™ How-to Guide *(cont.)*

Using the Text Tool

1. Select the Text tool from the toolbar.

2. Select the desired text size.

3. Press anywhere on the screen that you would like text to appear.

4. Type the desired text.

5. Select the Cursor tool and grab the text to move it around the page, if desired.

2.

4.

SMART Notebook™ How-to Guide (cont.)

Using Dual Page Display

1. Select the Dual Page Display icon from the toolbar. The screen will divide in half, and the current page will be displayed on the right.

2. Press the arrow to advance the current page to the left. The next page will appear on the right. The two pages can now be viewed and manipulated side-by-side.

1.

SMART Notebook™ How-to Guide *(cont.)*

Pinning Pages

1. Select the Dual Page Display icon from the toolbar. The screen will divide in half, and the current page will be displayed on the right.

2. Press the arrow to advance the page you want to be pinned until it appears on the right side of the display.

3. Select the Pin Page tool from the toolbar. This will pin the current page displayed on the left.

4. If you do not have the Pin Page tool on your toolbar, use the computer to select **View** from the main toolbar menu and then select *Zoom* from the **Pull-Down** menu.

5. Then select *Pin Page* from the second **Pull-Down** menu. This will pin the current page displayed on the left.

1.

3.

5.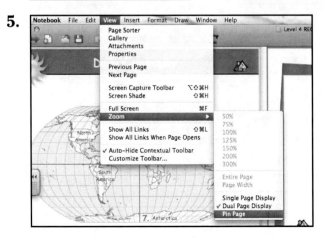

SMART Notebook™ How-to Guide *(cont.)*

Using the Cell Shade

Note: The cell shade only works when using a table.

1. When viewing a table file on a computer, right-click in the cell into which you want to insert the cell shade.

2. Select **Add Cell Shade** from the **Pull-Down** menu. The cell shade appears.

3. To remove the cell shade, select the Cursor tool from the toolbar and then press the cell shade with your finger.

4. When viewing a file on the interactive whiteboard, use the mouse buttons on the front of the interactive whiteboard to right-click in the cell into which you want to insert the cell shade. Then repeat steps 2 and 3.

SMART Notebook™ How-to Guide *(cont.)*

Using the Screen Shade

1. Select the Show/Hide Screen Shade tool from the toolbar. A screen shade will appear on the entire screen.

2. Adjust the size of the screen shade by dragging the top or sides of the shade.

3. To reveal the hidden information, drag the desired portion of the screen shade slowly.

4. To remove the shade completely, press the red circle in the top-right corner of the shade.

1.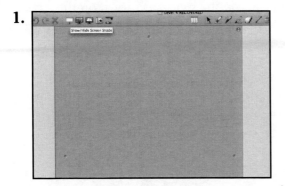

2.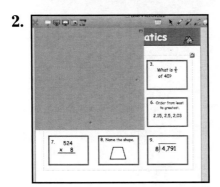

SMART Notebook™ How-to Guide *(cont.)*

Using the Spotlight Tool

1. Select the Spotlight tool from the toolbar. To turn on the Spotlight tool, select the Customize Floating Tools icon located at the bottom of the vertical toolbar. Then select **Other Interactive Whiteboard Tools** and then *Spotlight* from the **Pull-Down** menu. The screen will go dark except for a single circle.

2. To change the size or location of the circle, grab and drag the spotlight, using any black portion of the screen.

3. To change the shape of the spotlight, select *Shape* from the **Pull-Down** menu on the spotlight shown on the screen. Choose the desired shape from the second **Pull-Down** menu that appears.

4. To change the transparency of the background, select *Transparency* from the **Pull-Down** menu on the spotlight shown on the screen. Choose the desired transparency from the second **Pull-Down** menu that appears.

4.

Appendix B

ActivInspire™ How-to Guide

Customizing the Toolbox

1. Select the *ActivInspire* menu from the top of the screen and choose *Preferences* from the **Pull-Down** menu. The Edit Profiles window will open.

2. From the **Pull-Down** menu in the upper-left corner, choose *At The Board*. This will allow you to configure the toolbox that you will see when standing at the Promethean board.

1.

2.

ActivInspire™ How-to Guide (cont.)

Customizing the Toolbox (cont.)

3. Scroll through the menu of options on the left to choose command icons that you would like in your toolbox. To move a tool to your toolbox, simply click on the tool in the left column and then click on the **Add** button to add it to your toolbox.

4. To remove a tool from your toolbox, click on a tool in the right column that you would like to remove. Then click the **Remove** button to remove it.

3.
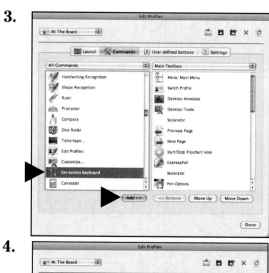

4.
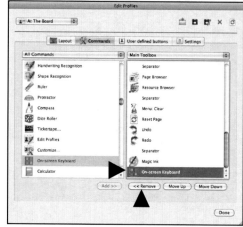

ActivInspire™ How-to Guide (cont.)

Customizing the Toolbox (cont.)

5. The following tools should be added to your toolbox for use with this book:

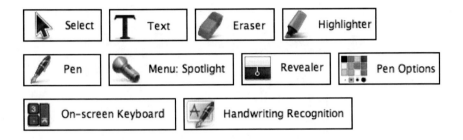

Advancing pages

1. When in slide show view on the interactive whiteboard, press the advance arrow on the toolbox.

2. If you want to move to the previous page, press the backward arrow.

3. To return to the home menu, press the house icon on the top of the page.

    1. and **2.**    **3.**

ActivInspire™ How-to Guide *(cont.)*

Saving a File

1. When viewing a file on a computer, select **File** from the menu across the top of the page.

2. Then select ***Save***.

1. and 2.

ActivInspire™ How-to Guide (cont.)

Dragging Objects or Text

1. Choose the Select tool from the toolbox.

2. Press the pen on the desired object or piece of text.

3. Without lifting your pen, drag the object or text to the desired location.

1. **3.**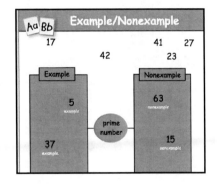

Using the Eraser Tool

1. Select the Eraser tool from the toolbox.

2. Choose the width of the eraser by using the width slider under the color palette.

3. Use the Eraser tool like a regular eraser to delete the desired annotation objects (Pen and Highlighter). *Note:* The eraser will remove all annotations, including those made with the Highlighter tool.

1. **3.**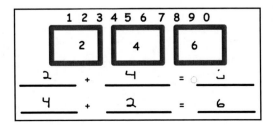

195

ActivInspire™ How-to Guide (cont.)

Using the Highlighter Tool

1. Select the Highlighter tool from the toolbox.

2. Select a color for your highlighter from the color palette.

3. Highlight desired text by dragging the pen over the text.

1.   2.

Using the Pen Tool

1. Select the Pen tool from the toolbox.

2. Select a color and line width from the menu by using the color palette and the line buttons and width slider.

3. Write or draw using the pen.

1.   2.

ActivInspire™ How-to Guide *(cont.)*

Using the Text Tool

1. Select either the Handwriting Recognition tool or Text tool and the On-Screen Keyboard.

2. Use the Select tool to grab the text and move it around the page, if desired.

Using the Zoom Tool

1. Select the **View** menu from the top of the screen and choose *Page Zoom* from the **Pull-Down** menu.

2. Press the pen to the board and hold it down, and the page will zoom to that location. Pressing the pen down again will reveal a hand icon that allows you to move around the page.

3. Tap the screen twice with the pen to restore the page to its original settings.

4. Then, choose the Select tool to get out of *Page Zoom*.

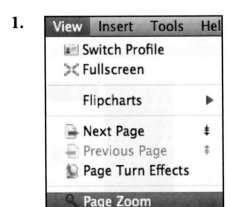

ActivInspire™ How-to Guide (cont.)

Using the Revealer Tool

1. Select the Revealer tool from the main toolbox. A Revealer will appear on the entire screen.

2. The Revealer is a toggle switch. Reveal hidden object(s) by clicking and dragging the blind from the top, bottom, right, or left.

3. To reveal the hidden information, drag the desired portion of the revealer slowly.

4. To remove the revealer completely, press the pop-out menu in the top-right corner of the shade and select **Close**.

1.   2. and 3.

4.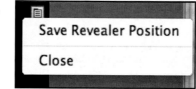

ActivInspire™ How-to Guide (cont.)

Using the Spotlight tool

1. Select the Spotlight tool from the main toolbox. Choose the type of spotlight from the **Pull-Down** menu (circular, square, circular solid, or square solid). The screen will go dark except for the spotlight.

2. The chosen spotlight can be:

   - moved by dragging any part of the masked area.

   - sized by dragging any part of the perimeter of the spotlight.

   While the spotlight is showing, you can continue to interact with any visible areas of the flipchart.

3. To change the shape of the spotlight, press the pop-out menu on the spotlight and select the desired shape.

4. To change the transparency of the background, select **File** and then **Settings**. Select *Effects* from the menu on the left to change color and translucency settings for the spotlight tool.

1. and **3.**

Appendix C

Internet Resources

Sources for eBooks

Website	Web Address
American Literature (free) Free online books of all the favorite classics, like *White Fang*, *Treasure Island*, and *Little Women*	http://www.americanliterature.com
Children's Storybooks Online (free) Illustrated children's stories for kids of all ages	http://www.magickeys.com/books
International Children's Digital Library (free) Search the database by age, reading level, language, genre, or interest	http://en.childrenslibrary.org
Reading A–Z (subscription) Leveled readers that students can have read to them, read on their own, and take a quiz on	http://www.readinga-z.com
Storyline Online (free) Favorite celebrities read books aloud	http://www.storylineonline.net
Story Place (free) Choose English or Spanish; interactive preschool and elementary titles	http://www.storyplace.org
Teacher Created Materials Interactiv-eBooks bring curriculum to life. Site licenses available.	http://www.teachercreatedmaterials.com/technology/interactiv-eBooks

Internet Resources (cont.)

Language Arts Websites

Website	Web Address
International Reading Association: ReadWriteThink.org Interactive reading and writing literacy activities	http://www.readwritethink.org/classroom-resources/?tab=2#tabs
Starfall Primary phonics and reading activities for young learners	http://www.starfall.com
PBS Kids Activities by subject and grade level	http://pbskids.org/whiteboard
Scholastic Web and whiteboard activities by grade level and subject	http://www.scholastic.com/teachers/student-activities
Sheppard Software Hundreds of online games, activities, and quizzes	http://www.sheppardsoftware.com
Vocabulary Games Games that build vocabulary skills	http://www.vocabulary.co.il

Internet Resources *(cont.)*

Mathematics Websites

Website	Web Address
Dream Box Learning Online Manipulatives	http://www.dreambox.com/teachertools
Fun Brain Arcade-like games to challenge students' mathematical skills and reasoning	http://www.funbrain.com/kidscenter.html
Hooda Math A site devoted to interactive whiteboard math games	http://hoodamath.com/games/iwb.php
Math Playground Choose from a list of concepts for interactive math lessons and manipulatives	http://www.mathplayground.com
A Maths Dictionary for Kids Online interactive math dictionary	http://www.amathsdictionaryforkids.com/dictionary.html
National Council of Teachers of Mathematics: Illuminations Hundreds of lessons and activities for PreK–12 math educators	http://illuminations.nctm.org
National Library of Virtual Manipulatives Choose from number and operations, algebra, geometry, measurement, or data analysis and probability at grades pre-K–2, 3–5, 6–8, or 9–12	http://nlvm.usu.edu/en/nav/vlibrary.html

Internet Resources *(cont.)*

Website	Web Address
The Teacher's Guide (Interactive Whiteboards) Choose a skill; lists suggested grade levels	http://www.theteachersguide.com/InteractiveSitesMathSmartBoard.htm
Thinking Blocks Model and solve math word problems	http://www.thinkingblocks.com

Internet Resources (cont.)

Science Websites

Website	Web Address
BBC Numerous simple science activities for ages 5–11	http://www.bbc.co.uk/schools/scienceclips/index_flash.shtml
BrainPOP and BrainPOP Jr. (both require a subscription) Information, short movies, activities, quizzes, and more	http://www.brainpop.com/science http://www.brainpopjr.com/science
Froguts Virtual Dissections Virtual dissection and lab software	http://www.froguts.com
National Geographic for Kids Games, videos, information and pictures about animals, news, and more	http://kids.nationalgeographic.com/kids
PhET Free physics, chemistry, biology, Earth science, and math interactive simulations	http://phet.colorado.edu
Scholastic Activities for grades K-10; life and Earth science and Investigations	http://teacher.scholastic.com/whiteboards/sciencemath.htm
Try Science Experiments, field trips, and adventures	http://www.tryscience.org
PBS Building Big	http://www.pbs.org/wgbh/buildingbig
The Jason Project The Coaster Creator	http://www.jason.org/digital_library/4851.aspx

Internet Resources *(cont.)*

Social Studies Websites

Website	Web Address
GameQuarium Economics games	http://www.gamequarium.com/economics.html
Google Earth Virtually visit any place in the world	http://www.google.com/earth/index.html
Google Maps Practice map skills	http://maps.google.com
iCivics Games and simulations related to civics	http://www.icivics.org
PBS The Democracy Project	http://pbskids.org/democracy
Reach the World GeoGames offers world geography activities	http://www.reachtheworld.org/games/geogames/index.html
Time for Kids Interactive digital editions of this weekly classroom news magazine are available	http://www.timeforkids.com

Internet Resources Cited

Audacity®. http://www.audacity.sourceforge.net.

BBC. http://www.bbc.co.uk/schools/scienceclips/index_flash.shtml.

BrainPOP. http://www.brainpop.com.

Children's Storybooks Online. http://www.magickeys.com/books.

Econopolis. http://library.thinkquest.org/3901.

Encyclopedia Britannica for Kids. http://kids.britannica.com.

Froguts Virtual Dissections. http://www.froguts.com.

Glogster. http://www.edu.glogster.com.

Google Earth. http://www.google.com/earth/index.html.

Google Maps. http://maps.google.com.

iCivics. http://www.icivics.org.

Inspiration® Software, Inc. http://www.inspiration.com.

The Interactive Whiteboard Revolution. http://iwbrevolution.ning.com.

International Children's Digital Library. http://en.childrenslibrary.org.

Internet4Classrooms. http://www.internet4classrooms.com.

Learning Today. http://learningtoday.com/corporate/reading-games.asp.

NASA. http://www.nasa.gov.

National Geographic for Kids. http://kids.nationalgeographic.com/kids.

Internet Resources Cited *(cont.)*

PBS The Democracy Project. http://pbskids.org/democracy.

Prezi. http://prezi.com.

Reach the World "GeoGames." http://www.reachtheworld.org/games/geogames/index.html.

Reading A–Z. http://www.readinga-z.com.

ReadWriteThink. http://readwritethink.org.

Shape It Up. http://www.kineticcity.com/mindgames/warper.

SMART™ Technologies. http://smarttech.com.

Starfall. http://www.starfall.com.

The Story Place. http://www.storyplace.org.

Storyline Online. http://www.storylineonline.net.

Visual Fractions. http://www.visualfractions.com.

YouTube. http://www.youtube.com.

References Cited

Ainsworth, Larry. 2007. "Common Formative Assessments: The Centerpiece of an Integrated Standards-Based Assessment System." In *Ahead of the Curve: The Power of Assessment to Transform Teaching and Learning*. Edited by Douglas Reeves. Bloomington, IN: Solution Tree.

Asher, James A. 2000. *Learning Another Language through Actions*. Los Gatos, CA: Sky Oaks Productions.

Bangert-Drowns, Robert, Chen-Lin Kulik, James Kulik, and Mary Teresa Morgan. 1991. "The Instructional Effect of Feedback on Test-like Events." *Review of Educational Research* 61 (2): 213–38.

Bender, William N. 2008. *Differentiating Instruction for Students with Learning Disabilities*. Thousand Oaks, CA: Corwin Press.

Boushey, Gail, and Joan Moser, "the sisters." 2006. *The Daily Five: Fostering Literacy Independence in the Elementary Grades*. Portland, ME: Stenhouse Publishers.

British Educational Communications and Technology Agency (BECTA). 2003. "What the Research Says about Using ICT in Maths." Accessed Oct. 26, 2011. https://www.education.gov.uk/publications/eOrderingDownload/15014MIG2799.pdf.

Brookhart, Susan M. 2008. "Feedback That Fits." *Educational Leadership* 65 (4): 54–59.

Catalanello, Rebecca. 2010. "Textbooks Ditched at Clearwater High as Students Log On to Kindles." *Tampa Bay Times*, June 2. http://www.tampabay.com/news/education/k12/textbooks-ditched-at-clearwater-high-as-students-log-on-to-kindles/1099264.

CCP Interactive Blog. 2011. "Interactive Whiteboards and iPads in the Classroom." *Complete Classroom Press*, June 21. http://ccpinteractive.blogspot.com/2011/06/interactive-whiteboards-and-ipads-in.html.

Cogill, Julie. 2008. "Primary Teachers' Interactive Whiteboard Practice Across One Year: Changes in Pedagogy and Influencing Factors." EdD thesis, King's College, University of London.

Collier, Virginia P. 1987. "Age and Rate of Acquisition of Second Language for Academic Purposes." *TESOL Quarterly* 21:617–41.

Conklin, Wendy. 2010. *Applying Differentiation Strategies: A Teacher's Handbook*. Huntington Beach, CA: Shell Education.

Corcoran, Elizabeth. 2009. "Getting to the Top of the Class." Forbes, October 5. http://www.forbes.com/forbes/2009/1005/technology-smart-technologies-getting-to-top-of-class.html.

Educational Service District 112. 2011. "The Sustainable Classroom." Accessed October 10. http://www.esd112.org/edtech/sustainableclass.cfm.

Enhancing Education. 2011. "Additional Teaching and Learning Strategies." Accessed October 18. http://enhancinged.wgbh.org/research/additional.html.

Fisher, Douglas, and Nancy Frey. 2008. *Better Learning Through Structured Teaching: A Framework for the Gradual Release of Responsibility*. Alexandria, VA: Association for Supervision and Curriculum Development.

Fleming, Neil. 2012. "VARK: A Guide to Learning Styles." Accessed August 28. http://www.vark-learn.com.

Florida Department of Education. 2011. "Executive Summary." Accessed October 10. http://www.fldoe.org/GR/Bill_Summary/2011/SB2120.pdf.

Folse, Keith S. 2005. "Vocabulary Myths: Applying Second Language Research to Classroom Teaching." *TESL Reporter* 37 (2): 1–13.

Gardner, Howard E. 1993. *Frames of Mind: The Theory of Multiple Intelligences.* New York: Basic Books.

Genesee, Fred, Kathryn Lindholm-Leary, William M. Saunders, and Donna Christian. 2006. *Educating English Language Learners: A Synthesis of Research Evidence.* New York: Cambridge University Press.

Glover, Derek, and David Miller. 2001. "Running with Technology: the Pedagogic Impact of the Large Scale Introduction of Interactive Whiteboards in One Secondary School." *Journal of Information Technology for Teacher Education* 10 (3): 257–77.

Hattie, John, and Helen Timperley. 2007. "The Power of Feedback." *Review of Educational Research* 77 (1): 81–112.

Hollie, Sharroky. 2011. *Culturally and Linguistically Responsive Teaching and Learning: Classroom Practices for Student Success.* Huntington Beach, CA: Shell Education.

Honey, Peter, and Alan Mumford. 1992. *The Manual of Learning Styles.* London: Peter Honey Publications.

Hunter, Madeline. 1982. *Mastery Teaching.* Thousand Oaks, CA: Corwin Press.

Jensen, Eric. 2008. *Brain-Based Learning: The New Paradigm of Teaching.* Thousand Oaks, CA: Corwin Press.

Kluger, Avraham N., and Angelo DeNisi. 1996. "The Effects of Feedback Interventions on Performance: A Historical Review, Meta-Analysis, and a Preliminary Feedback Intervention Theory." *Psychological Bulletin* 119 (2): 254–84.

Kolb, David A. 1984. *Experiential Learning: Experience as the Source of Learning and Development.* Upper Saddle River, NJ: Prentice-Hall.

Leite, Walter L., Marilla Svinicki, and Yuying Shi. 2010. "Attempted Validation of the Scores of the VARK: Learning Styles Inventory with Multitrait–Multimethod Confirmatory Factor Analysis Models." *Educational and Psychological Measurement* 70 (2): 323–39.

Lewis, C. S. 2001. *Mere Christianity.* San Francisco: HarperSanFrancisco.

Lobel, Arnold. 1979. *Frog and Toad Are Friends.* New York: HarperCollins Publishers.

Logsdon, Ann. n.d. "Multisensory Materials and Techniques." About.com. Accessed October 6, 2011. http://learningdisabilities.about.com/od/instructionalmaterials/p/mulitsensory.htm.

Marzano, Robert J. 2003. *What Works in Schools: Translating Research into Action.* Alexandria, VA: Association for Supervision and Curriculum Development.

———. 2009. "Teaching with Interactive Whiteboards." *Educational Leadership* 67 (3): 80–82.

Marzano, Robert J., Debra J. Pickering, and Jane E. Pollock. 2001. *Classroom Instruction that Works: Research-Based Strategies for Increasing Student Achievement.* Alexandria, VA: Association for Supervision and Curriculum Development.

McEntyre, Mandy. 2006. "The Effects Interactive Whiteboards Have on Student Motivation." Research Synthesis, University of Georgia. Accessed October 17, 2011. http://mandymc.myweb.uga.edu/iwb%20synthesis.pdf.

Miller, David, Derek Glover, and Doug Averis. 2004. *Enhancing Mathematics Teaching through New Technology: The Use of the Interactive Whiteboard.* Keele University Department of Education. Accessed October 18, 2011. http://www.

nuffieldfoundation.org/enhancing-mathematics-teaching-interactive-whiteboard.

Popham, James. 2008. "The Assessment-Savvy Student." *Educational Leadership* 66 (3): 80–81.

PR Newswire. 2011. "World's First Solar Powered Interactive Whiteboard Brings 21st Century Learning to Rural African Students." PR Newswire, February 10. http://www.prnewswire.com/news-releases/worlds-first-solar-powered-interactive-whiteboard-brings-21st-century-learning-to-rural-african-students-115708399.html.

SMART™ Technologies. 2005. "Jennings School District Case Study, St. Louis, Missouri." http://www.teq.com/downloads/documents/jennings.pdf.

———. 2006. "Interactive Whiteboards and Learning: Improving Student Learning Outcomes." http://smarttech.com/whitepapers.

———. 2009a. "Creating Classrooms for Everyone: How Interactive Whiteboards Support Universal Design for Learning." http://downloads01.smarttech.com/media/research/whitepapers/interactivewhiteboardsanduniversaldesignforlearningjan20.pdf.

———. 2009b. "Reducing Stress in the Classroom: How Interactive Whiteboards and Solution-Based Integration Improve Teacher Quality of Life." http://downloads01.smarttech.com/media/research/whitepapers/reducing_stress_wp.pdf.

———. 2011. "SMART Solutions: The Natural Way to Collaborate." http://smarttech.com/Solutions/Business+Solutions.

Solvie, Pamela A. 2004. "The Digital Whiteboard: A Tool in Early Literacy Instruction." http://www.readingonline.org/electronic/RT/2-04_column.

Somekh, Bridget, Maureen Haldane, Kelvyn Jones, Cathy Lewin, Stephen Steadman, Peter Scrimshaw, Sue Sing, et al. 2007. "Evaluation of the Primary Schools Whiteboard Expansion Project—Summary Report." Accessed October 12, 2011. http://downloads01.smarttech.com/media/research/international_research/uk/becta_executive_expansion_summary.pdf.

Stansbury, Meris. 2010. "New Projectors Make Any Wall an Interactive Whiteboard." eSchool News, January 13. http://www.eschoolnews.com/2010/01/13/new-projector-makes-any-wall-an-interactive-whiteboard.

Stiggins, Rick. 2007. "Assessment for Learning: An Essential Foundation of Productive Instruction." In *Ahead of the Curve: The Power of Assessment to Transform Teaching and Learning*. Edited by Douglas Reeves. Bloomington, IN: Solution Tree.

Stiggins, Rick, Judith Arter, Jan Chappuis, and Steve Chappuis. 2006. *Classroom Assessment for Student Learning: Doing It Right—Using It Well*. Portland, OR: Educational Testing Service.

Swan, Karen, Jason Schenker, and Annette Kratcoski. 2006. "The Effects of the Use of Interactive Whiteboards on Student Achievement." Kent State University. Accessed October 17, 2011. http://edtech2.boisestate.edu/spechtp/551/07_The_Effects_of_the_Use_of_Interactive_Whiteboards_on_Student_Achievement.pdf.

Teich, Annie. 2009. "Interactive Whiteboards Enhance Classroom Instruction and Learning." NEA Member Benefits, May 13. Accessed October 17, 2011. http://www.neamb.com/home/1216_2782.htm.

Tomlinson, Carol Ann. 2001. *How to Differentiate Instruction in Mixed-Ability Classrooms*. Alexandria, VA: Association for Supervision and Curriculum Development.

Wiggins, Grant. 1998. *Educative Assessment: Designing Assessments to Inform and Improve Student Performance.* San Francisco, CA: Josey-Bass.

———. 2007. "What Is an Essential Question?" Big Ideas: An Authentic Education e-Journal, November 15. http://www.authenticeducation.org/bigideas/article.lasso?artId=53.

Wiggins, Grant, and Jay McTighe. 1998. *Understanding by Design.* Alexandria, VA: Association for Supervision and Curriculum Development.

30229016379322
372.242 KOP
Kopp, Kathleen.
Using interactive whiteboards
in the classroom /